Edward Wall

EUROPE:
UNIFICATION
AND LAW

PENGUIN BOOKS

Penguin Books Ltd, Harmondsworth, Middlesex, England
Penguin Books Inc., 7110 Ambassador Road, Baltimore, Maryland 21207, U.S.A.
Penguin Books Australia Ltd, Ringwood, Victoria, Australia

—

First published 1969

—

Copyright © Edward Wall, 1969

—

Made and printed in Great Britain
by C. Nicholls & Company Ltd
Set in Monotype Times

PELICAN BOOKS

EUROPE: UNIFICATION AND LAW

Born in Croydon in 1908, Edward Wall was educated at Whitgift and Cambridge, where he read modern languages. On leaving university he joined the staff of the King's School, Canterbury, as senior modern languages master, and was later appointed a housemaster. While at Canterbury he began serious studies of European questions – the Central and East European minorities, the Spanish Civil War. By the mid-1930s he was engaged on the reorganization of the B B C schools broadcasts in modern languages and had started reading for the Bar, to which he was called in 1941. When war broke out he was put in charge of the selection and training of broadcasters for the European Service of the B B C and also broadcast regularly himself in French and German. But, holding a commission, he left in 1942 to join the forces and was posted to the Intelligence Corps; he served in North Africa and subsequently in Italy and in London.

After the war his already wide knowledge of European questions, and his linguistic expertise, were further developed into specialization in international legal questions. He was a founding editor of the *International Law Quarterly*, and for many years Honorary Secretary of the Society of Comparative Legislation and International Law, becoming, when that society merged with the Grotius Society, a member of the Council of Management of the resultant new British Institute of International and Comparative Law. Over the last twenty years, besides his ordinary work, he has many times lectured on English Law in France, Italy, Germany and Belgium. He has also broadcast from London in French and German, and has contributed many articles to legal periodicals as well as to Chatham House publications. His previous book, *The Court of Justice of the European Communities: Jurisdiction and Procedure* (1966), was greeted both as an authoritative work and as a pioneering endeavour in interpreting continental European legal thinking in a specialized field.

Contents

Introduction

A FEATURE of life in most countries of the world today is the greatly increased and still increasing control by government of the everyday affairs of the governed. Aspects of daily life, in respect of which government was formerly content to be a mere onlooker, have become its immediate concern, or have passed into its indirect (and frequently direct) control. In the democratic world it is not wholly involuntarily that the phenomenon has been brought about and is intensifying – though no doubt this has by no means always been done deliberately or fully consciously. But, as decision-making has thus passed increasingly from the governed into the hands of government, it is not surprising that in recent years the adequacy of the participation by the governed in the processes of this decision-making has been called in question. 1968 has been a year in which, in a variety of countries and in a variety of ways, that question has been searchingly posed.

Do there exist better methods than we have yet devised whereby the collective will is to be formulated – whether in industrial management or in local or national affairs? Do there exist better methods for implementing the decisions of the collective will, once it has been formulated? And, if that will is to be exercised for the maximum possible benefit of all who comprise the group (individuals and associations of individuals alike) how is that maximum benefit to be insured, or even defined, unless individuals are afforded the greatest possible participation in the processes of decision-making? Is it not true, in fact, that the tendency for these processes to be removed from their reach is enhanced precisely in the degree, and at the time, that human affairs become the concern or pass into the control of groupings or collections of individuals (the 'collectivity') and out of the unhindered control of individuals themselves?

Answers to questions such as these can hardly be found in the abstract, that is to say without reference to the circumstances and the organization of the collectivity, or grouping, or society – however it be looked upon – in which they arise. The concern of this book is with the organization and the circumstances of the new forms of human grouping that European unification has brought or is bringing into being, and within which, more as a matter of international than national or purely local affairs, corresponding questions present themselves. To put it another way, the central theme of this book is new forms of government and the relation in which individuals, and their associations, stand to them.

These are matters which have confronted the creators of the new Europe as practical issues. In attempting to solve them they have in many respects built anew. But since what they built has perforce to be superimposed on the old, the characteristics of the latter could not be merely disregarded. This preoccupation with both the old and the new is reflected in the present book. It aims at describing, though in necessarily somewhat summary form, principal areas of law, both in the individual nation States and in the new European groupings, which affect the lives of all who dwell within them.

By what constitutional rules do these nations and groupings respectively cohere? What are the relationships within them between executive power and legislative power? And what of the separability of these two from each other, or of the third governmental power, that of the judiciary, from both of them? By what systems of administrative law is the exercise of executive power within the nations and groupings controlled? How is the ordinary law that prevails in individual nation States affected by increasing cohesion between these States themselves (even if criminal law remains an essentially national affair)? What of the sovereignty and independence of these States as their cohesion increases? What – for many perhaps the most important query – of the legal position of the individual, and of his participation in decision-making, in this whole process? These are some of the questions in respect of which the following pages offer suggestions and seek to promote discussion.

This is a subject at the very heart of the human story, and law – which this book is about – is life itself.

1

Historical Outline

FROM earliest times, whenever the instinct of self-preservation led individual human beings to seek protection in numbers, the grouping thus formed was inevitably confronted with the problem of government. Who was to give the orders that all must obey? Who was to ordain how the grouping was to be organized, whether in peace or war? By whom, and in accordance with what principles, were disputes between the members of the grouping to be settled? The government of men has always required the exercise of these three forms of authority, or power. We have become accustomed, in the last two hundred years or so, to speak of them as the power of the Executive, of the Legislature, and of the Judiciary, respectively. If not as old as the hills, they are certainly as old as the earliest forms of human society. One and the same individual might exercise all three forms of authority; he might be Ruler, Law-giver and Judge combined. Until comparatively recently, he frequently was. Whether he were Chief, Count, Duke, King, Tsar, Maharajah or Shah, to govern was then to exercise each and all of them.

In such circumstances there would be no impediment to arbitrary government, where it was willed, except the ultimate resistance of the governed. Yet if that point were reached, the whole operation must be seen as broken down, and failure confessed. For a society without government is no viable society. With what heart-searching and hesitations, therefore, must many of the English barons and prelates, in the thirteenth century, have inscribed the document they were to place before King John. For it was not breakdown of the social structure that they wanted; their aim, even if they barely formulated it, was to bring central government within the dimensions of custom and accepted law, and so, by Magna Carta, to outlaw the arbitrary. It seems it was not lightly done.

Henceforward – in however elementary a sense, and though the word was not used – central government was to be 'constitutional'. In certain matters there was now a declared order; the law stood revealed. The prior and more exacting task had been to discern and shape the requisite order; there followed the elaboration of the law to give it rational expression. But as always in human affairs, when law and order are established, the two were affirmed simultaneously.

The outlawing of the arbitrary exercise of power is no more than a beginning of constitutional government. Indeed it is rather a preliminary to it, than a beginning of it. For the direct concern of constitutional law is with the lawful exercise of power rather than the unlawful.

As the human grouping progresses, to become a wider society, or, eventually, a nation, containment of the exercise of governmental power within the agreed constitutional bounds will inevitably involve a growing discernment and clarification of the three forms it may take – executive, legislative and judicial. Not only that, but the agreed manner of their interaction will become constitutionally established.

Containment within agreed bounds of the exercise of governmental power is only one side of the coin. A constitution, like a coin, has another. And each side is the converse of the other. For to define the bounds of government is, at the same time, to prescribe rights and liberties for the governed. Or vice versa.

The nature of the rights and liberties of the governed are the hallmark of the society to which they belong. They express its quality. Of what avail is it if the instinct for self-preservation should lead men to subscribe voluntarily to an order of society in which the twin instinct for self-fulfilment is denied expression? Their rights and liberties, like a hallmark, may be unobtrusive; there may be no need repeatedly to assert them. But they are fundamental. Upon their existence there depends ultimately the kind of life that men may lead. Consequently, part of the duty that all men owe to maintain the society in which they live is to pay the price of eternal vigilance for their defence.

In the tangled skein of the last thousand years of European history, there is particular fascination in seeking to trace the threads by which the different human groupings of which Europe is composed arrived at the constitutional order which they each know today. In most of the western part of the continent, and in the United Kingdom and Scandinavia, there is now a broad similarity in the positions they have reached. The basic human liberties are vouchsafed – though the procedures vary by which they may if necessary be asserted. Everywhere the three forms in which governmental authority may be exercised are conceived in distinction one from the other – though the constitutional arrangement for the interplay of Executive, Legislature and Judiciary varies somewhat from one human grouping to another. From the concept with which they started, of unitary and absolute power in the hands of a single individual ruler, all have progressed to the position they now occupy.

Absolute power is not necessarily arbitrary. In France, the practice had early gained hold for the King to take counsel before he acted. The practice became customary law. By the late thirteenth century, the King's free choice of counsellors had become restricted, so that he was bound to seek advice either from persons of rank (such as barons, prelates or other great dignitaries), in the kingdom and at court (the 'Curia Regis'), or from professional jurists. A formal name was given to the system in 1303, when the expression Great Council (Grand Conseil) was first used. There were alternative names – 'Conseil privé', 'Conseil secret' and others. Even in the time of Louis XIV, when the practice of absolutism was at its resplendent height, the coins and medallions were stamped with a permanent reminder of the essential principle of French monarchy: 'Nil nisi consilio'.

Within the Council, the task of the professional jurists was to examine and assess all matters brought before it, so that action upon them might readily be taken. Illogically, they were also members of the Parlement. This, the body in which men 'had deep speech' together – a deliberative assembly, as we might now think of it – began as a part of the Curia Regis, the King's Court. By the thirteenth century it had freed itself from attendance on the King, and, while the Great Council would move from place to place with him, the Parlement remained in Paris. The illogicality becomes startling paradox with the realization that it was against this very Parlement, and the independent legislative and judicial power that it acquired, that, with the steady support of the Great Council, the Kings of France were fated to conduct for centuries a relentless and tenacious struggle – the Executive at war with other arms of government.

The same word 'Parlement' came into use in England in the thirteenth century. Two hundred years earlier, so says the Chronicle, William the Conqueror had had 'very deep speech with his Witan'. Later, 'colloquium' or 'parlement' came to mean, first, a debate; then, a formal conference. In England, as in France, a Great Council took shape. In 1275 the Statute of Westminster designated it 'Parlement'.

This was a period when English constitutional history might easily have taken the same course as that of France, and absolutism have been the outcome. The distinction of the Executive from the other arms of government had become more marked by the formation of an official body to service its operations, which was separate from the rest of the Council. The two might have hardened into their separate moulds, had they not been prevented from doing so by the hostility of barons and prelates to the King; by his defeat in battle in 1264; by the scheming and ambitious Simon de Montfort; by the plan advanced by de Montfort for a pattern of government in which there should exist a thorough 'parliamentary' control over the Executive. The Statute of Westminster not only laid part of the foundations for the supremacy which Parliament was fully to acquire four centuries later. Perhaps equally important, it aimed at ensuring that the three distinct arms of Government should operate, not separately, but in constant interplay as different functions of one whole.

Two divergent trends – towards absolutism, or away from it – were thus early revealed by the examples of France and England. Two threads in the tangled skein of European history. Within the next four to five hundred years, as each of the human groupings of Europe moved into more modern cohesion, glimpses of these trends show up in the skein. In Spain, for example, there was the failure of the Cortes to acquire control over the executive power, in the way the English Parliament was progressively doing. In the Netherlands, there was the wresting by the people, in the fifteenth century, of the 'Great Privilege' from the ruler of Burgundy.

Frequently alluded to as the Dutch 'Magna Carta', this might conceivably have been followed by further constitutional developments similar to those witnessed in England, had the advantages thereby won not had to be surrendered to later foreign rulers. Geographical exposure to the south and east always made the Netherlands a relatively easy prey to foreign domination. Yet, in the States General, the country early developed a distinct legislative body, standing over against, though never encompassing, the executive authority of the Stadholders, who were the lieutenants of the royal power. It was, indeed, the uneasy relationship between these two forms of authority that was the main cause of no less than five revolutions in the 200 years of the 'Dutch Republic' (1580–1790).

In the seventeenth century, while continental Europe was being shown, and tending to imitate, the heightened absolutism of France, England was putting further touches at that time to a constitutional order which should finally eradicate its possibility (though, in Britain in the 1960s, random if powerful voices can be heard to suggest, not without cogency, that Cabinet government as it has latterly developed, presents the danger that the power of the Executive is no longer truly encompassed and controlled by the Legislature).

By the eighteenth century, continental Europe had its 'enlightened despots'. Philosophical and legal ideas were in ferment. The clear distinction between the three forms of governmental authority was, for one thing, becoming more widely appreciated. Montesquieu, setting his gaze on England, believed he there discerned that they were completely separated. That in fact they were distinct and interacting, rather than strictly separated, was largely overlooked in the profound and widespread influence that his writings enjoyed. There can now be hardly a constitution in any Western European country in which the trace of this influence is not evident, and today, as will be shown later in this book, the separation of powers is a much-discussed question in the constitutional law of the European Communities.

Not only the separation of the powers of government, but the reverse of the constitutional coin, the liberties and freedoms of the governed, was a matter with which continental Europe became increasingly preoccupied in the latter years of the eighteenth century. The famous French Declaration of the Rights of Man of 1789 presaged a continuance of that preoccupation throughout the nineteenth century, as the political geography of Western Europe was fashioned more nearly to the shape with which we are now familiar. As in a vast kaleidoscope, the human groupings of earlier times were now moving, over much of the area, towards larger units. A multiplicity of principalities and dukedoms, of minor republics and small kingdoms, were here to forgo a separate status. In North Western Europe, by contrast, as a result of separation from the Netherlands, Belgium and Luxemburg were to acquire it.

The nineteenth century was thus the century for the making of constitutions in Europe – all of them, unlike that of the United Kingdom, expressed in writing and usually in a single legal instrument. In each of these, the powers of government and the rights of the governed were given explicit expression – with increasing precision through the years as one or other constitution was successively amended. Upon this basis, the free way of life could develop, in the last thirty years of the nineteenth and into the twentieth century, in a fuller manner than that to which much of Europe had previously been accustomed. A more assured constitutional basis for individual liberties, a more precise determination of political and civic rights, an increased democratization of the political process (universal suffrage was becoming everywhere a recognized necessity) – these could not of themselves remedy the social and economic injustices which were all too apparent. But they provided the platform without which the remedy would anyway remain out of reach. Who can say whether it might not have come within the grasp of European civilization early in the twentieth century, had not human weaknesses and ambitions, a lack of vigilance, and a ruthless trampling on constitutions, together produced the two holocausts from the results of which it is now barely emerging? New platforms are now being built in Europe, so that the reach may go higher – but these are the concern of a later chapter.

The ferment of philosophical and legal ideas of the eighteenth century had been directed at more than the ideal constitutional law of any human society. Besides 'public law' – as the lawyers term it, because it is concerned with any given society as a whole, and the relationship between Government and governed within it – what occupied the legal thinkers of the eighteenth century was the need to codify the ordinary law and make it more homogeneous and accessible. The ordinary law – call it by whatever name you please: 'civil law' (as on the European Continent), 'common law' (or 'private law', as in England) – had been built up in continental Europe from a variety of sources. Roman law, canon law, Germanic law, custom and usage, some or all of these, according to the geographical area, had their part to play in regulating the relationships of individuals or groups of individuals to other individuals (or groups). How and when contracts are to be legally enforceable; when compensation for harm or injury done is to be payable; what rights a husband and father is to have in respect of his wife and family; how property is to be transferred or inherited – all these and many other such matters are primarily the concern of private law. Unless that law is clear and readily ascertainable, any human society will be uncertain of itself, and its everyday life disorganized. Codification of private law was much favoured in the eighteenth century, over the whole of continental Western Europe.

It was in the nineteenth century that codification was mainly brought about. The emergence at that time of the new nation States of modern Europe was frequently followed sooner or later by the emergence of a code of civil law – as, for example, in the case of Italy, Austria, Switzerland, Germany, and so on – and often by the emergence of a code of commercial law (and codes of procedural law) as well. The French civil code – which bears the name of Napoleon, and is said to have been regarded by him as the best monument to his régime that he could possibly have bequeathed – was the forerunner in much of this development which was sufficiently comprehensive for the impression to be gained that any political entity of human beings positively requires the formulation of a unified system of private law for them to follow.

Yet the union of Scotland and England into a political entity has not prevented the continued application and growth of their two very different systems of private law – still less has it positively necessitated their unification. One example will illustrate this. The law governing partnership – the relation which subsists between persons carrying on any trade, occupation or profession in common with a view to profit – developed gradually as a result of the decisions given by judges in individual cases. But development in England diverged from that in Scotland. Whereas in Scotland a partnership was itself looked upon for legal purposes as a unit (or, as the lawyers say, a 'person'), in England all legal questions concerning a partnership continued to be conceived and handled mainly in terms of its individual membership. In time, it was out of the law of partnership that company law emerged, and as it did so in the early nineteenth century, the principle of a company having a legal personality of its own quite distinct from that of each of its members (who, unlike members of a partnership, should have limited liability) was recognized in England and Scotland alike. Company law was early put into statutory form – by Act of Parliament that is – applicable to both countries, and successive 'Companies Acts' since that time have always been made to apply to Great Britain as a whole (while N. Ireland has a separate though similar statute). In all its main features, therefore, company law in England and Scotland is, and has long been, the same, whereas partnership law, at least in one important aspect, is not. Similarly, for many years before the Napoleonic codes, distinct systems of mainly customary law had operated in the northern and southern areas of unified France. And the treaties establishing the three European Communities, far from requiring the unified codification of the private law of the member States, do not even carry a mandate for its mere harmonization – except to the extent that this is necessary for the operation of the 'common market'.* It thus appears that in the twentieth century, as in the nineteenth, the effect on their private law of the merging of human groupings is at most indirect. If political integration does not positively require unification of all private law, a mere desire for academic tidiness is unlikely to bring it about, so that

---

*In 1962, when a draft treaty for the political Union of the European Peoples was under discussion by the six Common Market countries, one of the objectives for which the five delegations other than the French wished to

the only alternative impetus would seem to be any sheer inconvenience resulting from its absence.

Part of the security – part of the certainties in life – that men seek, consciously or unconsciously, from the grouping to which they belong, is afforded to them by a reliable system of private law to regulate their daily affairs. They are unlikely to have it continuously in the forefront of their minds or even to need to do so; but part of their security will lie in the realization not only that it is there to protect them when they need it; but also that it is sure and certain – at least to the extent that it is ever possible for law to be. That is their legal security. Its value is enhanced by the sureness of that law itself and of its essential spirit, as well as by its relative slowness to change the outward forms, legislative or judicial, in which it is expressed. In a dynamic society it must of course change, but any great and sudden alteration in the fundamental principles of the law of contract, for example, on the basis of which the everyday business of a whole people has been habitually conducted, would clearly throw them into a state of uncertainty and at least temporary disorganization. Other instances abound. Wherever there is a movement towards the unification of peoples – or of part only of their affairs – the more alert amongst them will look to their private law. What will be the direct commitments, or the indirect influences, to change it? How far does it safely shelter against extraneous influences, behind the constitution? By what constitutional processes may it properly be transformed in response to external commitments? For that matter, and quite apart from external commitments or influences, what is the process of law formation within any human grouping – in a word, how does law become law?

That is not a question that has a simple answer in respect of any single nation, let alone a uniform answer applicable to them generally. In England, upon the body of common law (private

---

make provision was 'the harmonization and unification of the laws (and of the legal institutions) of member States'.

It was agreed in the drafting committee that provision could be made for the Council of the Union to specify at a later stage the spheres in which it felt that harmonization or unification of laws was desirable. Negotiations for a treaty of political union came to a standstill later in 1962 (see Chapter 5).

law) built up over the centuries by the decisions of the judges declaring the law in individual cases, there are superimposed the statutory enactments of the Legislature (Acts of Parliament). These, coming with increasing frequency in modern times, also regulate private relationships. In western continental Europe, broadly speaking, the legislatures have long, if not always had the initiative in private law formation, though the consistent interpretation by courts of final appeal of the exact meaning of the law thus formed has also played a great part. Is the general answer to the question, then, that private law is formed in a manner resulting from the particular interplay of two of the three forms of government – Judiciary and Legislature – that is provided in any given constitution? Such an answer would have covered any of the situations existing in the various human groupings of Western Europe up to the beginning of the nineteenth century. As in some *pas de deux* these two – Judiciary and Legislature – were the principal dancers upon the stage of law formation. It was their varying and interrelated movements that gave enduring expression to basic rules of private law.

As the nineteenth century unfolded, a third dancer joined with increasing frequency in the dance, and, doing so, changed its nature. For then the law which the dance expressed was no longer merely private law. Its concern was with the legal relationships of private citizens, not as between themselves, but with governmental authority. The trend everywhere in Europe was towards administrative systems that were more and more centralized. It was towards positive activity by governmental authority in realms where its former role had been that of a bystander, or at most a supervisor. As society became more highly organized and administered, what had formerly been tacitly accepted as matters of purely private concern became also matters of public interest. What a man might do with his own had perhaps never been solely and exclusively his own affair. In any event, it was now becoming much less so. Society in general also had an interest. How far that interest should be legally enforceable, and how far the private citizen should have legal protection against the power of society to pursue it, these were the two related aspects of the new and growing law to which the *figure à trois* gave expression. In that dance, the initiative for each movement was with the Executive, the administrator. The alert spectator could observe that, in carrying each movement through, the Executive might tend to usurp and not merely inspire the role of the Legislature, or might take to itself the mantle and authority of the Judiciary.

This dance, said some spectators long familiar with the *pas de deux*, was something quite different. It was a new genre. This was not private law. It was public law – for the interest of all society was involved. Constitutional law might be public law *par excellence*, but for that matter, criminal law was also public law – and so, too, was the newcomer, administrative law.

As it progressively took on shape and form, there was correspondingly established, in greater or smaller degree in all Western European countries, a clear distinction between public law on the one hand, and private law on the other, as both potentially regulating (though not simultaneously) the rights and duties of private individuals and their associations, and the powers of the bodies representing governmental authority with which they had dealings. This is a distinction which similarly permeates the law of the European Communities (express reference to it being present in the treaties establishing them) so that an awareness of its nature is of importance for an understanding of the implications of that law. But to say this at this point is to anticipate by a century and a half a development in the present narrative. It was in France that the new concept, in the early nineteenth century, was the more apparent and readily definable.

The Grand Conseil, or Conseil du Roi, which had been concerned with administration, and not infrequently with the legal problems which it threw up, had of course been abolished in the Revolution, and for some time had not been replaced. But the Constitution de l'An VIII revived it in name and Bonaparte renovated it in practicability. It became the Conseil d'État, entrusted with advising the central government on administration and its legal aspects – and acting also, exclusively, as the judge in disputes between private rights or interests and those of the State. It may have been the liberalism of the nineteenth century that facilitated the establishment by the Conseil d'État of a body of case law that, today, gives the interests of private citizens more complete legal protection against those of the State than is probably to be found anywhere else. But it was the fact that it was a judicial institution separate from the system of ordinary civil and criminal law courts that caused the administrative law it developed to be looked upon more readily as a distinct genre.

From the fact of the separateness as a tribunal of the Conseil d'État, the fact of its being what the French call a 'juridiction spéciale', some foreign observers of the French scene deduced, more readily than the case law justified, that here was a body of law which favoured the State against the individual. It is now generally agreed that this was the error into which the great Professor A. V. Dicey fell. 'In Britain', he wrote in 1885, in his *Introduction to the Study of the Law of the Constitution*, 'no man is punishable or can be lawfully made to suffer in body or goods except for a distinct breach of law established in the *ordinary* legal manner before the *ordinary* courts of the land' (present author's italics). This was one of the main propositions of the Rule of Law as he propounded it. The Rule would obviously be breached if any 'juridiction spéciale' were to exist. Where it did exist, this by itself constituted an open invitation to deduce that the law it purveyed must have a particular slant. Indeed, when the Conseil d'État was established by Napoleon, part of the intention was to draw off from the ordinary courts all legal disputes between private interests and the State, so that a highly centralized administrative programme could go ahead less impeded. That the Conseil d'État succeeded in this, while at the same time evolving a body of law giving great protection to the individual, may be an accident of history – but it is one of the most important features in the French experience of government over the last 150 years.

That there were no similar separate courts in Britain to deal with disputes between private interests and governmental authority did not mean that administrative law could not there exist. The ordinary courts, as part of the Rule of Law, had methods at their disposal (in particular, the so-called Prerogative Writs) which enabled administrative disputes to be handled wholly adequately in the circumstances of the nineteenth and early twentieth century – though many doubt whether, even with changes made since 1945, they are adequate today.

In the Netherlands, too, it was to the ordinary courts, whose jurisdiction was specially extended for that purpose, that the constitution-makers of 1815 looked for the protection of individual rights against authoritarian rule. Belgium, becoming independent of the Netherlands in 1830, continued that tradition; but it did not prevent her ordinary courts from making use of a great deal of the administrative law that the Conseil d'État in France was evolving. It was not until 1946 that Belgium chose to establish a Conseil d'État with a disputes procedure on French lines. For the Netherlands, the possibility of following more closely the French system was opened up with a reform of her Council of State in 1861, by the addition of a 'disputes section'; but accidents of history, or of personalities, deflected her interest to German thinking on administrative law matters. In 1866, the Luxemburg Conseil d'État which had first been introduced into the constitution ten years earlier, was given a more decisive role as judge of administrative disputes. At about the same time the Consiglio di Stato of the newly independent Kingdom of Italy was launched on a course similar to that of the French body of the same name; within its somewhat more restricted ambit, the case law it has evolved touches common ground at many points with that of France. So when, in the nineteen fifties, the time came, and the force of circumstances required it, these six nations had no particular difficulty in finding sufficient common ground between all of them in this branch of law, and incorporating it as one of the most important elements within the new dimensions of the European Communities.

Back in the nineteenth century, legal dimensions such as these were not even imagined, perhaps largely because they would have far surpassed the requirements that then existed. There was in fact no challenge to the imagination to exert itself in this direction, no necessity which could mother such an invention. For there was as yet no recognizable need for the States of Western Europe to integrate their national lives – even in the economic sphere, let alone the political – into some form of international whole. Some of them, indeed, had barely attained statehood. Such problems of integration as had to be faced were national, not international. Diverse human groupings brought together to constitute single

States, were still, like Italy and Germany, in process of integration. There, as in other States newly come to independence, such as Belgium and Luxemburg, the order of the day was the fostering of nationhood. The efforts, outside their own countries, of the nationals of the various European States – in trade, exploration, research and invention, military endeavour, or Government – could no doubt be assessed, in political terms, as serving a general national interest. But except in war, they could only very infrequently be seen as contributions to any transcendent international purpose engaging the attention of any whole group of States on a common cause. For in peace time it was at most pairs of States, rather than groups, that shared in joint endeavours. Such endeavours were directed, moreover, towards achievements that were extraneous, and would leave the main stream of national life unaffected, however much they might redound to the credit of the individual nations, or improve their well-being. By contrast, Western Europe in the mid-twentieth century is feeling its way in endeavours of a group of States that have as their transcendent purpose the merging and integration of much of their individual national lives.

It was with the legal equipment of the nineteenth century that they stood at the threshold of this task. Entering upon it, they designed fresh equipment that might take the stresses and strains of the new dimensions – and the suitability of that design for its purpose is now undergoing, with considerable success, the harsh tests of experience. But, entering upon the new, they did not abandon the old. The nation States that brought certain aspects of their individual national lives into transcendent international community did not, by that act, go out of existence or make themselves redundant. In consequence, the law by which their national identity is defined, or which regulates and protects their national way of life, was not forsaken. Changed it will be, particularly in certain fields of private law, and that is the intention; proud constitutional law must condescendingly free the way for the entry upon the national scene of these new influences in private law; yet their effect will not be directly upon the fundamentals of the law of contract, for example; the effect will be to render unlawful in practice contracts that are restrictive of international competition within the Community; criminal law will not be touched, and other public law no more than slightly. The process which has now begun is one of deliberately fostered interaction between two systems of law, one old, one new, with the old committed in advance to modifications of itself as the result of the grafting upon it of the new. Such a process has not been witnessed before in international relations. To understand it requires some familiarity with those legal features which are common to all nation States, and which have heretofore conditioned the conduct of their international relations.

The nation State, its independence and sovereignty: these concepts which today underpin the world-wide transactions of mankind and form – to give a specific example – the basis for the operations of the United Nations Organization, took shape and were perfected in Europe. It happened gradually. The concepts now have clear legal meanings, or at least connotations, but the process out of which they were evolved was that of establishing, in a material sense, the political order to which the peoples of Europe could be brought at any given period of her history. It was the phenomenon that has already been referred to as revealing itself at the time of Magna Carta: the establishment of the order could be accompanied by discernment and declaration of the law to give it formal expression.

Sovereignty was thus the first of these concepts to evolve, because it could be personalized in the individual rulers who governed the human groupings of early times. As these human groupings consciously assumed nationhood a new concept began to emerge, though sovereignty could still remain personalized in the individual ruler. It does not seem, however, that the word 'sovereign' was actually used in this particular political sense until late in the sixteenth century. The attributes of political sovereignty in an individual ruler could be recognized and legally respected, without recourse to the word, though by the end of the Middle Ages it was used in France for an authority – political or other – which had no other authority above itself. England, as has been mentioned previously in this chapter, was early set on a constitutional course of containment of executive authority, which was to lead by slow degrees to what we now know as the sovereignty of Parliament. Sovereignty was thus early depersonalized, in England, though again, the word was not used. In France, it was introduced into political science by Bodin, whose celebrated work, *De la République*, was published in 1577. At the same time he gave a new meaning to it. Being influenced by the policy of centralization introduced by Louis XI (1461–83), the conscious founder of French absolutism, he defined sovereignty as 'the absolute and perpetual power within a State'. For him, no constitution could limit the sovereign's supreme power, which is above positive law, and subject to no restrictions whatever except the Commandments of God and the Law of Nature.

Constitutional containment of power, or no such containment – around this fundamental divergence of view was centred much of the legal and philosophical debate of the next two centuries. Around it, too, were centred the political struggles for which men gave their lives. It conditioned in large measure the history and fortunes of the peoples of Europe.

In time, all Western Europe was to come to the depersonalization of sovereignty, not only in practice but in terms of legal definition. It was no longer in a personal ruler but in the nation that it was seen to reside. Over the same period, nationhood, assisted by territorial demarcation, came increasingly to assume the guise and postures of statehood. The nineteenth century was to see the apogee of the nation State, and, from the point of view of its internal law, finally to conceive sovereignty as the highest underived power in the State and as the exclusive competence to determine the jurisdictional limits of that power. From the point of view of the relations of any one State with other States, what appeared to matter was the separate individuality of each. So independence became a legal definition for that aspect of the sovereignty of a State which is supreme authority, independent of any other earthly authority, in particular the authority of any other State. In international usage, sovereignty and independence, or sovereign independence, thus became co-related terms. They matched the requirements of international practice. In large measure they still do.

But, increasingly since the Second World War, the circumstances of scientific invention, ease of communications, and the facts of economics, have combined – in a manner too familiar to need description here – to make nation States act interdependently rather than independently. How does their established legal equipment – sovereignty, internal and external, independence, the law of the constitution, the procedures set up for dealing with questions of administrative law and for the modification of private law – how does this equipment safeguard the national way of life while facilitating, or conceivably hindering, the new, interdependent pattern of behaviour of both States and their nationals in Western Europe? It is with these matters that this book is basically concerned.

2

Surrender of Sovereignty?

IT is, of course, by treaties, international conventions and agreements, that a sovereign independent State enters into binding arrangements with other States, or with international organizations. International law requires that such binding arrangements shall be observed and duly performed – *pacta sunt servanda* – and the fact that in practice some are not is no more a proof of the non-existence of the law, than is the non-performance of a contract proof of the non-existence of a law of contract governing the private relationships between the members of any given human grouping.

But if a State is bound by law to observe and perform the international agreements into which it enters, then, many people ask themselves, does not this mean that every time a State enters into such an agreement it surrenders some of its sovereignty?

Surrender of sovereignty is a misleading phrase. For, in the first place, to enter freely and willingly into a treaty, or international convention or agreement, is an exercise, not a surrender, of sovereignty. In the second place, the State which enters into the arrangement frequently, if not always, agrees thereby to act in future in a certain way (though sometimes this may be only on the occurrence of a given contingency, as in the case of a defensive agreement to assist another State if attacked). By so agreeing it limits its freedom of action. But does it surrender its sovereignty, any more than an individual, who makes a binding contract with another, surrenders his individuality? The terms of that question are no doubt somewhat simpler than those required for an adequate answer – as will be shown – but it is a question fairly put, which warns against too facile talk of *surrender* of sovereignty.

The answer is best given by concrete examples. So, killing two birds with one stone, there now follows a brief survey of the treaties, international agreements and conventions, into which

Western European States including the United Kingdom have entered together since the Second World War (thereby promoting European Unification) and of the effect of their so doing upon their national sovereignty.

The European Convention of Human Rights (signed in Rome in 1950, and in the drafting of which the major share fell to United Kingdom delegates) makes it possible for any person over whom a State adhering to the Convention has jurisdiction, who considers that the rights guaranteed to him by that Convention are being infringed by that State, to carry his complaint to the European Commission of Human Rights set up by the Convention – provided he has first exhausted what lawyers call the 'local remedies', that is to say, the legal means available to him in the allegedly offending State for securing redress. If such a person can establish his case, within the procedures laid down by the Convention, the ultimate result can be that the Government of the offending State becomes obligated to put right the matter complained of.

It is perhaps not important that the number of cases in which persons will be able to bring about that result may be small; it *is* important that a system such as this should have been introduced, adding a new international dimension to the upholding of human rights in any country ratifying the Convention. But does a State's acceptance of the system amount to partial surrender of its sovereignty? By the fact of acceptance nothing is taken away from the existing executive, legislative or judicial power of the State in respect of persons within its jurisdiction; these functions of sovereignty may continue to be exercised just as before. Only if the State so uses its sovereignty that oppression is the consequence may a course of action be imposed upon it by a new-dimensional authority. Seen in its proper light, adherence by a State to the Convention means, not a surrender of its sovereignty, but the exclusion, from the exercise of that sovereignty, of all acts which are contrary to human rights as defined in the Convention.

For the United Kingdom – where individual rights and liberties are, for the most part, not defined in positive terms – there is some novelty in being party to a convention in which they are thus defined. But that the novelty effects no vital substantive change in British law is surely amply demonstrated by the fact that no parliamentary Statute has been found necessary to implement the Convention. Nothing was being taken away from it, or – substantively – added to it. The Crown could assume externally its obligations under the Convention without any disturbance of the internal situation.

Why, indeed, should the Convention of Human Rights have been thought necessary? Much of the answer is to be found in two principal paragraphs of the preamble to the Convention, signed in Rome on 4 November 1950 by the United Kingdom Government and the governments of thirteen other member States of the Council of Europe.* They agreed on the terms of the Convention, 'Considering that the aim of the Council of Europe is the achievement of greater unity between its members and that one of the methods by which that aim is to be pursued is the maintenance and further realization of Human Rights and Fundamental Freedoms', and 'Reaffirming their profound belief in those Fundamental Freedoms which are the foundation of justice and peace in the world and are best maintained on the one hand by an effective political democracy and on the other by a common understanding and observance of the Human Rights upon which they depend'. To an understanding and observance of Human Rights some of the signatory countries had come early in their history, particularly the United Kingdom; others had done so only recently, after many vagaries, if not in their understanding of them, certainly in their observance of them. This was the historical moment to seek to guarantee by collective international action the legal basis of a free society over a wide area of Europe, thereby promoting, in one form, its unity.

Here was one of the earliest expressions of the new Europeanism. Over Western Europe, ravaged and exhausted by war, had spread the recognition, like the waxing light of a fresh dawn, that for the new generation the attitudes of mind, and the hopes and aspirations which now united them, transcended by far the national feelings which for centuries had divided them. And there had come, too, with a passionate determination to put a final end to

* Austria, Belgium, Denmark, Germany, Greece, Iceland, Ireland, Italy, Luxemburg, Netherlands, Norway, Sweden and Turkey.

the nationalist rivalry and internecine war which had ravaged Europe for so long, a keen desire to benefit from a larger economic market and technology on an international scale. For the new generation recognized that unless this were achieved the European nations must reconcile themselves to the fact that they would remain for ever second class industrial powers.[*]

For a free society to flourish, its legal security alone does not suffice. There must also be, in the first place, physical security for that society. Just as, behind their protective legal moat, individual liberties and an increasingly secure free society had evolved in Britain, so, sheltered by the encircling seas, had physical security been protected since 1066 from the invader. There must secondly be economic security, or at least viability, for that society: Britain has always had to ensure her economic security in large part by her overseas trading activities – activities which have also led, incidentally, to the transplanting overseas, in many countries of the world, of the common law under which the liberties of Britain had flourished at home. And, according to the degree of national economic security attained, there may be added, thirdly, so much social security for individual inhabitants as national economic strength can sustain – as the British Welfare State testifies.

In continental Europe, similarly, legal security on a collective basis for a free society has been matched by collective arrangements for defence and for improvement of economic well-being, while a European Social Charter has also been drawn up by the Council of Europe. One of the earliest post-war European treaties was the Brussels Treaty 'of Economics, Social and Cultural Collaboration and Collective Self Defence', signed on 17 March 1948. In the preamble to this treaty the Heads of State of Belgium, France, Luxemburg, the Netherlands and the United Kingdom expressed their resolve

to reaffirm their faith in fundamental human rights, in the dignity, and worth of the human person and in the other ideals proclaimed in the Charter of the United Nations; to fortify and preserve the principles of

[*]See the speech by Edward Heath, then leader of the Opposition in the British Parliament, at Harvard, U.S.A. 21 March 1967.

democracy, personal freedom and political liberty, the constitutional traditions and the rule of law, which are their common heritage; to strengthen, with these aims in view, the economic, social and cultural ties by which they are already united; to cooperate loyally and to co-ordinate their efforts to create in Western Europe a firm basis for European economic recovery: to afford assistance to each other ... in maintaining international peace and security and in resisting any policy of aggression ...

Enlarged in 1954 to include Western Germany and Italy, since when it has been known as Western European Union, this treaty, it will have been noted, is directed to all the four forms of security mentioned above, which a free society requires in order to flourish: legal, defensive, economic and social. Again, though it requires its participating States to exercise their sovereignty in certain ways, and so may be seen as excluding its exercise in ways that are incompatible therewith, it cannot be regarded as a treaty necessitating *surrender* of sovereignty by any such State.

Within a few weeks of the signing of the Brussels Treaty, there was created the Organization for European Economic Co-operation, by a Convention signed in Paris on 16 April 1948. This was in response to the famous speech of General Marshall at Harvard in June 1947, inviting the European countries to draw up an agreed programme for economic recovery and promising American support in putting it into execution. In July of that year, after the British and French Governments had tried in vain to secure the collaboration of the Soviet Union and its satellite States, an economic conference was convened in Paris which was attended by all non-communist countries in Europe except Spain. After further negotiations, a permanent Organization for Economic Cooperation was decided upon, and was established by the Convention just mentioned. Unlike the Brussels Treaty, which created very little international machinery for carrying out its purposes, the Convention established an international organization, whose aim it defined as 'the achievement of a sound European economy, through the economic cooperation of its members'. However, it placed the responsibility for promoting the various measures of economic cooperation, not upon the organization as such, but on the States signing and ratifying the Convention.* Nevertheless, it marked a considerable advance on earlier methods of inter-State cooperation, by conferring upon the Council of the organization the power to take decisions which were binding on the member States. Here was to be seen, not surrender of sovereignty, but a clear acceptance of an obligation to exercise it, for certain purposes, under direction from an international body.

Just a year after the O.E.E.C. there was established another form of European cooperation. This was the Council of Europe (the Statute of which was signed in London on 5 May 1949, and later amended in 1951, 1953 and 1958). It was the Consultative Council of the Brussels Treaty Organization which had promoted the new body, in the formation of which five other countries (Italy, Ireland, Denmark, Norway, Sweden) were invited to join.† This was indeed to be a new type of international body, or institution, consisting of a ministerial committee meeting in private, and a consultative assembly meeting in public. 'There is need of closer unity between all like-minded countries of Europe', the preamble to the Statute affirmed, and 'it is necessary forthwith to create an organization which will bring European States into closer association.' The first article of the Statute strikes the same note as had already been sounded in the Brussels Treaty:

The aim of the Council of Europe is to achieve a greater unity between its members for the purpose of safeguarding and realizing the ideals and principles which are their common heritage and facilitating their economic and social progress...

But it then goes into some detail as to how this is to be achieved:

This aim shall be pursued through the organs of the Council by discussion of questions of common concern, and by agreements and common action in economic, social, cultural, scientific, legal and administrative matters, and in the maintenance and further realization of human rights and fundamental freedoms.

*The number of these was increased to 18 with the admission of Spain in the summer of 1959. The U.S.A. and Canada became associate members.
† Further accessions followed: Greece, 9 August 1949; Iceland, 7 March 1950; Turkey, 13 April 1950; the Saar, 13 May 1950; Western Germany, 15 July 1950; Austria, 16 April 1956.

It has already been seen how the last named became the subject of its own special Convention. But human rights and fundamental freedoms are by no means the only field in which the Council of Europe has been active. In twenty years of life its member states have concluded upwards of sixty European-conventions, covering social affairs, public health, culture and education and legal questions. Treaty-making is by no means all it has done. Since 1966 the inter-governmental activities of the eighteen member States have comprised a programme of work covering some 150 headings.

Outstanding conventions have been the European Social Charter, the European Cultural Convention and a number of agreements concerning university studies, social security, patents, establishment, the peaceful settlement of disputes, extradition, travel without passports, insurance of motor vehicles, mutual assistance in criminal matters, copyright in the exchange of television programmes and facilities for medical exchanges, notably in connexion with blood plasma and therapeutic substances of human origin. The European Pharmacopeia was established in Strasbourg in 1966. The Council has also been active in the campaign for European nature preservation, and has agreed to a European Water Charter, designed to preserve European waterways and keep pollution in check.

In this context, and in the whole field of regional planning, it has been assisted by a biennial European conference of local authorities which has met in Strasbourg, and has reported to the Consultative Assembly and, through that body, to the Committee of Ministers.

In the strictly legal and administrative field, the Council has benefited since 1960 from meetings, every two years, of a European Conference of Ministers of Justice. These meetings have considered the following aims: the harmonization of national laws, with a view to greater European unity; the establishment of an improved legal order between member States, and the highest possible degree of equality before the law for citizens of a member State on the territory of another State; consolidation to that effect of impending national legislation; a certain measure of joint preparation in national legislation; joint measures for the prevention of crime and treatment of offenders, including the co-ordination of criminological research.

European conventions on Establishment, relating both to individuals and to companies, have been completed, and there have been further conventions on foreign money liabilities and their place of payment, and the international transport of animals; a European Consular Convention, and the recognition and enforcement of arbitral awards. In the legal field, as in other specialist activities, the inter-governmental work of the Council has been conducted by a Committee of leading legal experts, assisted by a qualified European Secretariat. Its task has been to review proposals for conventions, to draft such conventions for approval and signature by the Committee of Ministers and to prepare the work of the European Conference of Ministers of Justice.

An important innovation in recent years has been a working agreement between the Council of Europe and the European Community in Brussels, with a view to the better coordination of work between the two bodies and the preparation of conditions, notably in the legal field, whereby countries other than the Six may find it easier to join the European Community in the future. Since the Six also belong to the Council of Europe, this means that they too participate in tasks designed to promote greater unity between member States, tasks which fall at present outside the Six-Power Treaties of Paris (1951) and Rome (1957).

By January 1960 it was clear that the time had come to review developments to date in Europe's economic relations. The original purpose of O.E.E.C. had largely been fulfilled, and six Western European countries had inaugurated their 'common market' in 1958. Seven others were, by the progressive abolition of tariffs between themselves, seeking advantages similar to those which the Six were obtaining by the same process behind the protection of an encircling external tariff which was common to them all. These last two developments had led the associate members of O.E.E.C. – the U.S.A. and Canada – to a much-increased interest in the European market. The changed circumstances and the new potential scope for O.E.E.C. resulted in its transformation into more of an Atlantic than a purely European body, under the name 'Organization for Economic Cooperation and Development'. The United Kingdom remained a member of this body. It had also been a prime mover in the formation of the European Free Trade Area and, since 1961, has been seeking membership of the common market (and the two other Communities) established by the Six.

The treaties establishing these three communities are (from the purely legal point of view) of a different and more novel kind than any of the other European treaties and conventions of the last twenty years which have just been passed rapidly in review. The latter were arrangements for common or concerted action in various fields of endeavour, depending ultimately for their success on the collaboration of member states (even where, as in O.E.E.C. and the Council of Europe, they established centralized Institutions, in the form of inter-ministerial Councils with power to take decisions binding on all the member States). But the three community treaties were arrangements not merely for *collaboration*, even if under the direction of a central institution, but for positive *integration* of large areas of the economic and social life of the member States. What, then, of their sovereignty and independence? How were these affected?

Here again there has been much facile talk of 'surrender' of sovereignty. The true answer is more complex, and can really only be arrived at by examining the mechanisms by which the treaties are made to operate within the individual member States (as is done in the following chapter). But in general it is fair to say that these treaties have caused a blurring of the conventional theoretical line dividing those affairs of a nation which are internal, from those which are external, and that with this change there has come about a change in the manner in which sovereignty is exercised over those national affairs which, from their former positions, have moved in either direction over the dividing line.

Like the other European treaties just referred to, the Community treaties are concerned with the freedom of man, his economic well-being, his social security. The methods envisaged, the concepts employed, may be more sophisticated and complex.

But, fundamentally, the quest is the same: to project on to a wider territorial area than that of any single nation State, the opportunities to practise the basic freedoms and possibilities for assured and creative living of which, until the last twenty years, the nation State was the only legally constituted guarantor or provider, and within that wider area to establish on an international basis the underlying constitutional guarantees for those basic freedoms and possibilities. Economic expansion, the growth of employment and a rising standard of living, upon the basis of the free movement, across national frontiers, of persons, services, capital and goods – these were the main goals to be achieved under the direction of a centralized executive power subject to completely independent judicial control, as well as, in the last resort, to the checkmate of an international Parliamentary Assembly.

In such a balance of the three forms of governmental power (though in the Communities that of the Parliamentary Assembly is less to the fore than in a democratic nation State) it is easy to recognize the constitutional formula which the western democracies, with some variants, had come by experience to rely upon as the guarantee of individual liberties. 'Community' is an apt word to describe what is, though not a State akin to a nation State or to the result of a merging of several such into one, a form of embryonic international or regional society, with its own constitution and laws, in which men's lives can develop in liberty in a new dimension, yet without loss of their various national allegiances, patriotisms, and systems of security.

Within this new form of society the Community exercises its own sovereignty, through its executive, judicial and parliamentary institutions. The sovereignty which it exercises is the sum total resulting from deliberate pooling by its member States of certain of the functions of their own individual sovereignties, which until the establishment of the Communities, they had reserved strictly to their own use. This matter is discussed somewhat more fully in Chapter 3. But, from the moment of its establishment, each Community, like a ship leaving harbour, is propelled by the exercise of the pooled sovereignty thus conferred upon it, and enjoys, in law, a wholly independent existence. It evolves its own legal order, which, for all that its provisions are enforceable within the individual member States, is none the less completely distinct and autonomous.

3

Community Law and State Law

'WE must be free or die, who speak the tongue that Shakespeare spake.' The truth of those words, tested over and over again in our earlier history, was never put to so severe a test, and proved to the very hilt, as in the Second World War. As close to death as it is possible to come and yet survive, we risked death rather than accept survival without our freedom. That is our deepest national instinct. What is this freedom which we so cherish – to the point, when roused, of passion?

It is the liberty of every citizen in the land to have a mind of his own – to think his own thoughts, to speak his mind, and also to move unimpeded from place to place as he wishes – provided only that in doing these things he acts lawfully. These things constitute his personal freedom; and he may lawfully enjoy it to the full, so long as in doing so he does not disturb the peace and good order of the society in which we live. Which is only another way of saying that he must allow others to enjoy precisely the same freedom as he does himself. It is we ourselves – more than any ruler, more even than any judge – who have created this, our freedom, and in doing so have built step by step the constitution under which we live.

Thus it was not always true that except a man be committed to prison by judgment of the Queen's Courts, or detained while awaiting trial by them, his immediate physical freedom could be secured by use of the famous writ of Habeas Corpus. In 1627 the executive Government imprisoned Sir Thomas Darnel and four other knights because they would not subscribe money for the King. When application was made to the Court of King's Bench for his release, it ruled that he could not be freed by Habeas Corpus because it was at the command of the King that he had been sent to prison.

But, through their Parliament, the people of England overthrew the government which would so curtail their liberties. Laws were passed establishing the writ of habeas corpus in the form in which we know it today – as a writ obtainable by any person on behalf of the prisoner, as well as by the prisoner himself (an important safeguard, though in practice every facility is granted to a person in prison to make application for the writ).

Never since that time have the judges, at the behest of the executive arm of government, connived at a man being unlawfully deprived of his liberty. Even in the tensest moments of the Second World War, when, for the safeguarding of the ultimate freedom of us all against the activities of suspected enemy agents within the land, Parliament (by Regulation 18B, under the Emergency Powers Act) had given power to the Minister to detain any man whom he had reasonable cause to believe to be of hostile origin or of hostile associations, so that it was necessary to control him – even in those tense moments, the instinctive revulsion of Englishmen against the imperative war-time necessity for the grant of such a power of imprisonment, was voiced in a great dissenting judgment. While a majority of the Law Lords felt they had no alternative to deciding that the wording of the Regulation made it impossible for the courts of law to review the exercise of the power by the Minister, Lord Atkin was moved to declare:

In this country, amid the clash of arms, the laws are not silent. They may be changed, but they speak the same language in war as in peace. It has always been one of the pillars of freedom, one of the principles of liberty for which we are now fighting, that the judges are no respecters of persons, and stand between the subject and any attempted encroachment on his liberty by the executive, alert to see that any coercive action is justified in law. In this case I have listened to arguments which might have been addressed acceptably to the Court of King's Bench in the time of Charles I. I protest, even if I do it alone, against a strained construction put on words with the effect of giving an uncontrolled power of imprisonment to the Minister.*

It was in the time of Charles I, of course, that Sir Thomas Darnel had in vain sought habeas corpus of the court. That was in 1627. Only two years later the same thing happened again. A

*Liversidge v. Sir John Anderson (1942) Appeal Cases, p. 244.

silk merchant of London, one Richard Chambers, had been thrown into the Fleet prison by the Court of Star Chamber, and sought release by habeas corpus from the Court of King's Bench, who refused to grant it. The ground on which he asked for it was that the Star Chamber had no power to punish him merely for words he had used. What he had actually said was: 'The merchants are in no part of the world so screwed and wrung as in England', and he had used these words when called to the Council Board at Hampton Court to explain complaints about the conduct of customs officials. The Star Chamber fined him £2,000 for what he had said and ordered him to confess his wrong. But he refused. Never till death, he said, would he acknowledge any part of it. As a result he spent six years in prison. But in 1641 the Star Chamber was abolished and by the time of the Commonwealth, Richard Chambers had lived to became an alderman and sheriff of the City of London. He had indeed done much for the freedom of every man to have a mind of his own – to think his own thoughts, to speak his mind. But most of all he had demonstrated, as had Darnel, that there could be no liberty so long as the judges did the bidding of the executive government. It was his determination, together with that of Darnel and of others, which established the fundamental constitutional principle of the independence of the judiciary. Since the second half of the seventeenth century it has stood as firm as a rock.

More still required to be done to establish the freedom of mind and speech. To the judge's independence of the executive there needed to be added the jury's independence of the judge – particularly in cases where the court had to decide whether a man's words were unlawful because they disturbed the peace and good order of society. For a man's words hardly ever convey exactly the same meaning to every one of his listeners or readers. Partly according to the individual state of mind of each of them individually, his meaning will vary; there is a large subjective element in the assessment of other people's meaning. Better, therefore, that a jury of twelve (in Scotland fifteen) rather than a judge alone, for all his independence and objectivity of mind, should judge a man's words.

'Sir,' said Junius in an open letter to King George III, 'it is the misfortune of your life, and originally the cause of every reproach and distress which has attended your Government, that you should never have been acquainted with the language of truth, until you heard it in the complaints of your subjects.' In 1770 the printer of those words was tried before Lord Mansfield and a special jury of the City of London on a charge of sedition – or, more technically, seditious libel. Lord Mansfield instructed the jury that whether the words were libellous or not was a question of law for the judge to decide; the jury had only to decide whether the paper was printed and published. (There can be no libel without publication, for a man's words spoken only silently in the recesses of his own mind, are not known and can cause no immediate harm to others.) Since the answer to the second question was patently obvious, the judge was in effect instructing the jury to find the accused man guilty. But the jury did not do so.

Half the population of London were assembled in the streets surrounding Guildhall, and remained several hours expecting the result. Lord Mansfield had retired to his house, and many thousands proceeded thither in grand procession when it was announced that the jury had agreed. At last a shout, proceeding from Bloomsbury Square and reverberating from the remotest quarters of the metropolis, proclaimed a verdict of not guilty.*

The battle was won; not only since Fox's Libel Act of 1792 can no judge prevent a jury exercising its right to give a general verdict of guilty or not guilty (or, in Scotland, as a third alternative, not proven) but the freedom to criticize the government, provided the words used are not seditious, was established – by the people themselves.

By the people themselves, that is to say by the dogged, non-violent, determination of individuals to take their stand on a principle that their instinct told them was right. Whether through Parliament, whether through their jurymen, and always by their own vigilance, that was how the liberties of Britons – with far less violence than was used by other peoples – were acquired, clarified and established.

Since the common law, thus evolved, gave to every man the maximum of freedom compatible with that of others, there was

*Lord Campbell: *Lives of the Chief Justices*, Vol. II, p. 489.

never any need for a comprehensive enumeration in positive terms of the liberties of the subject, contained, as in other democratic countries, in a single law of the constitution. Nor is it by such a single law of the constitution that individual liberties are guaranteed; for the guarantee lies in the rules of the common law and, equally important, the procedures by which these are upheld. A guarantee by single constitutional enactment was not required, given that, at intervals through the long course of British history, declarations of rights had been wrested from the Monarch (Magna Carta, 1215, the Great Charter of the Liberties of England and of the Liberties of the Forest, 1297, and the Bill of Rights, 1689, are, of course, the outstanding examples) and the arbitrary power of the Crown restricted. Put together with the common law, these occasional charters provided the broad foundations upon which there has flourished in Britain as secure a legal order for society, coupled with unquestioning enjoyment of civil liberties, as has probably ever been seen in the world. Whether it be personal freedom or freedom of the mind, or any of the other freedoms at the root of which lie these two, the story is the same. Out of the instinct and vigilance of the people there have been vouchsafed to us, in our generation, freedom of conscience, freedom of public worship, freedom of assembly and association, equality before the law, the right to free elections, freedom of property, family rights, the right to work and to withhold one's labour, freedom of the press, and many other freedoms.

Freedom of the press, that great instrument through which vigilance can express itself and caution us of danger to our liberties (as it also can through broadcasting), is itself an outstanding example of how these result, in the main, not from positive legal conferment (as do the rights inscribed in the great historical charters) but simply from the absence of any law to prohibit their exercise. For at one time, under the Licensing Act, 1662, printing was a monopoly and was only permitted under licence; but since 1695, when the Act was not renewed, the freedom of the press has consisted in printing without licence, subject to the limitations of ordinary law.

From all the foregoing, there has now emerged a picture – incomplete in detail, but realist rather than impressionist – of the

41

legal aspect of the British way of life. A body of law progressively constructed over centuries, which we may call our constitution, a derivative from, rather than a guarantee of, individual liberties; a body of law containing such inbuilt rules – whether of contract, tort, or crime – as are necessary to protect that way of life from abuse or disruption, no more, and certainly neither the result of overweening government nor affording the opportunity for the exercise of such; yet, a body of law over which a freely elected and non self-perpetuating Parliament stands supreme; a body of law, finally, the public administration of which is entrusted – so far as litigation is concerned – to what by European continental standards would appear to be a mere handful of judges – not recruited in early manhood into a lifetime judicial career, for no such possibility exists, but drawn in middle life from amongst practising members of the Bar (who number at the present time, in England and Wales, no more than 2,500 in all, and who alone have a right of audience in the High Court). Judges and barristers, together with solicitors, who constitute the other branch of the legal profession (and besides fulfilling an indispensable role in the preparatory work of any case litigated in the courts, conduct a vast amount of non-litigious legal transactions on behalf of their clients) operate the system of administration of justice. It is a system firmly rooted in independence – in the sense, that is, not only of complete independence from Executive and Legislature, but of that sturdy individual independence compounded of character, intellectual stamina and moral fibre which the system inevitably fosters in those who administer it and which may be seen as the counterpart of the sturdy quality of the individual British citizen who himself has done so much to establish the law. That, within these islands, is, legally conceived, how we live.

And, as if encircling this citadel of freedom, there is a great protective moat, with Parliament commanding the drawbridge, so that, unless it is lowered, no treaties or agreements entered into with powers external to the realm can take effect within so as to modify the rights and liberties of the denizens.

Treaties and agreements with foreign powers are not made by Parliament, but by the Queen, and her Ministers on her behalf. In order that the legal results of such treaties and agreements may enter into and form part of the body of law sheltered by the moat, Parliament must first lower the drawbridge – it must approve such internal results of exterior action. Normally, its approval given, it will implement these by the means always at its disposal, legislation by Statute. Theoretically, therefore, there is a potential hiatus between the external acceptance of a national obligation and internal fulfilment of the obligation so accepted. But in practice Parliament is consulted, the sense of the electorate gauged, before the Queen and her Ministers finally commit the nation to external obligations such as these.

Even such an international agreement as that (1944) establishing the International Monetary Fund, which might at first impression be supposed to be solely concerned with the country's external relationships, needed to go through this procedure so that Parliament might implement its internal effects by special legislation. But if the procedure, intentionally, has not been followed, nothing will avail the foreign litigant seeking to enforce an alleged right, derived from international treaty or agreement, by ordinary process of law in the courts of this country, against a defendant protected by the moat. So, in 1950, the Italian Government could not succeed against Hambro's Bank in the Chancery Division of the High Court (on a claim based on an inter-governmental Anglo-Italian financial agreement entered into for the purpose of settling up the wartime financial account of the two nations) when it attempted to secure from the bank the policy monies (derived from assurances effected in England) of King Victor Emmanuel whose personal estate the new Italian Constitution of 1947 had confiscated. There had been no parliamentary approval, even implicit, of the inter-governmental financial agreement; the drawbridge had never been lowered; and a private right to assets, behind the moat, even though the right of an alien, could not be prevailed against in the ordinary courts. It was only on the international plane that the inter-governmental agreement could operate; it could not touch individual private rights acquired within the United Kingdom.

Clearly, however, if the United Kingdom were to become a member of the European Communities, Parliament would have to lower the drawbridge, because, if for no more general reason, the treaties on which the Communities are based (as well as much of the legislation of the Communities implementing the treaties) have a direct bearing on private rights.

Such an action on the part of Parliament would, of course, be in exercise of its sovereignty; that is, of its supreme authority within the State. For in the constitutional edifice that has been slowly erected over the years, that is the position Parliament occupies. As early as 1589, Sir Thomas Smith, Secretary of State of Queen Elizabeth, defined the supremacy of Parliament as follows:

The most high and absolute power of the realm of England consisteth in the parliament ... That which is done by this consent is called firm, stable and *sanctum*, and is taken for law. The Parliament abrogateth old laws, maketh new, giveth orders for things past and for things hereafter to be followed, changeth rights and possessions of private men, legitimateth bastards, establisheth forms of religion, altereth weights and measures, giveth forms of succession to the crown, defineth of doubtful rights, whereof is no law already made, appointeth subsidies, tailes, taxes, and impositions, giveth most free pardons and absolutions, restoreth in blood and name as the highest court, condemneth or absolveth them whom the prince will put to that trial. And, to be short, all that ever the people of Rome might do either in *centuriatis comitiis* or *tributis*, the same may be done by the parliament of England which representeth and hath the power of the whole realm, both the head and body. For every Englishman is intended to be there present, either in person or by procuration and attorneys, of what preeminence, state, dignity or quality soever he be, from the prince, be he king or queen, to the lowest person in England. And the consent of the parliament is taken to be every man's consent.

Sovereignty is not omnipotence, though, legally speaking, there is nothing that Parliament cannot do. But the proper procedures must be observed, and it should never be overlooked, moreover, that 'Parliament', as the supreme legislative body, consists of the Queen (whose final assent is required before a Bill becomes a Statute) together with the two Houses, of Lords and Commons.

Parliamentary sovereignty is almost exclusively concerned with internal matters in the State, and is not coextensive with State sovereignty, for the treaty-making power does not belong to it. State sovereignty, however, in internal affairs, manifests itself in and through Parliament. For whilst sovereignty and independence confer upon a State both liberty of action in intercourse with other States, and liberty of action inside its borders, it is a matter of the constitutional law of any particular State, how the latter liberty is exercised. In the United Kingdom it is through the sovereign body of Parliament.

The decision whether it is desirable to lower the drawbridge lies with the Executive arm of government in the first place; but whether it is in fact lowered depends upon the Legislature, who must therefore also be convinced of its desirability. But though such interplay between two arms of government – that is, two of the three powers of sovereignty – demonstrates the distinct existence of both, it is clear that in practice they are not distinctly separable. Moreover, whatever the position in law as to their separability, it is the size of the majority which the political party forming the Executive (the 'Government') enjoys in the Legislature (Parliament – to which the Executive also belongs and to which it is responsible), that determines, in all but an exceptional case, not only the practical liberty of action of the Executive but the degree of its identity of interest with the Legislature.

The Judiciary. the third of the three sovereign powers, is, however, clearly independent of the other two. But, in the mid-twentieth century, is its indirect role in the building of the constitution, in the way that has been described, now at an end? Is the common law to develop slowly still further, or to remain static, as if photographed in its posture of this moment of history? Is Statute Law to be so preponderantly the operative law of this country that the independence of the Judiciary will be manifested no longer in the creation of law, but only in the *interpretation* and *application* of law that it cannot itself create, let alone oppose? In any event, it appears clear that if the drawbridge is lowered in welcome to the law of the European Communities, the role of the Judiciary, in relation to that new law, will be primarily one of application and only in a limited sense one of interpretation – since the final arbiter in matters of interpretation will be the Court of Justice of the Communities.

If the circumstances of the mid-twentieth century are accelerating the change in the role of the Judiciary, making much more obvious the shift of emphasis that was already beginning to be felt fifty or more years ago, they have also produced, like some *deus ex machina*, a form of ultimate international guarantee of individual liberties that before the Second World War would have been well-nigh inconceivable – in the shape of the European Convention on Human Rights, which was discussed in the preceding chapter.

Within Britain, in the twentieth century, it is not the legal (or constitutional) basis of individual liberties that has suffered any direct threat of principle. Rather have the actual opportunities for their full exercise been subjected to increasing limitations imposed on all by the State itself – imposed by the collective will of all individuals on individuals themselves, for, as Sir Thomas Smith put it in 1589, '... the consent of the parliament is taken to be every man's consent.' It is at that point that there exists a problem. It is at that point that vigilance needs to be exercised, because, particularly since the Second World War, by the will of the nation, expressed through Parliament, there have been conferred on the Executive an ever-increasing number of powers of interference with the private liberties and interests of individuals – or of associations of individuals. That has been (and is being) done for a purpose, and done constitutionally. There is no quarrel with that.

This problem does not result from the sheer volume of legislation nowadays introduced by the Government, from the consequent strains imposed on the mechanics of Parliament, or from the threat to its established procedures that these embody. The problem that is here of interest arises at the next stage: much of the legislation thus passed, intricate though it has to be, may nevertheless constitute no more than an outline within which a given policy or plan is to be carried out; furthermore not only may the details of its application, even in terms of a general programme, be more than the Statute itself can encompass, but there may well be a need for rapid changes to be made in its detailed application (as may arise, for example, from a sudden shift in economic trends or factors). Power must therefore be given to the Executive to legislate directly in respect of the details. What results is 'delegated legislation' as it is technically called, which may then be not merely regulatory, but positively interventionist –

that is to say, the Executive may either merely provide a framework of control limiting the sphere within which decisions that are economic (say) may be freely taken by the citizens or their associations, or it may in fact take the decisions itself.

There are three kinds of constitutional safeguards against the abuse by the Executive of such powers: Parliamentary, Political and Judicial.* But when the point has been reached at which a directly interventionist decision in respect of an individual, or an association of individuals, may be taken by the Executive, the moment for operating the parliamentary safeguard will have passed, and the individual, or the association, who considers himself unwarrantably prejudiced by the decision, is thrown back on the judicial safeguard. Indeed, the same is true in respect of a general framework of control established by the Executive in the exercise of powers conferred upon it by Statute.

The question therefore arises: How adequate is the system of administrative law, enforceable at the hands of the Judiciary, to control the *legality* of the exercise of administrative power by the Executive? (Clearly – at least as matters now stand – the courts can control no more than the *legality* of such an exercise, and can have no regard to whether it is expedient or opportune). There can be no doubt that in the last twenty years or so the British system of administrative law (though there are considerable differences between the English system and the Scottish – and also that of Northern Ireland) has been considerably strengthened. This is not the place to enter into a full description, but the outstanding importance must be mentioned of the Crown Proceedings Act of 1947, permitting recovery of damages from the Executive for tort or breach of contract (without the former necessity of obtaining leave of the Crown to sue) and of the Tribunals and Inquiries Act of 1958, whereby the courts can now exercise a wider control over the legality of two of the principal features of modern governmental administration.

Added to the existing framework, these new features provide a body of administrative law in Britain that, with less clarity of

---

*These are more fully discussed in Chapter 4, where they are compared with similar safeguards available in the constitution of the European Communities.

definition, is in substance, though not in the procedures for enforcing it, not too different from the system developed in the continental countries of Western Europe. One element that exists there, however, is still lacking in the British system: a method whereby the court can oblige the Executive to make use of a power duly conferred upon it, but which, to the detriment of members of the public, it is neglecting to use. Administrative law is a prominent feature of the European Communities, which, on the pattern familiar on the Continent, provide for full judicial control by the Communities' Court of Justice, of the legality of the exercise of their treaty powers by the Community Executive (either the Commission of fourteen members operating from Brussels, or the Council). There is sufficient similarity between the British and the Communities' system for there to be no particular difficulty for British lawyers in operating the system, should the United Kingdom join the Communities by signing and ratifying the treaties which established them. Yet, in the sphere of administrative law, it is likely they would have more to learn than to impart.

To return to the question of the impact of the community treaties upon the sovereignty of individual member States: with respect to the United Kingdom, this can now be examined upon the hypothesis that sooner or later that country will become a member.

In the first place, since the treaties are designed to take effect internally within each member State (and, in particular, contain provisions creating individual rights that can be enforced in the national courts by persons subject to their jurisdiction) it is obvious that Parliament would have to lower the drawbridge – to use the same image – so that to the body of law protected by the moat there is added a fresh body of law: community law. This addition would presumably be effected by the passing of a special Act of Parliament for the purpose. But it should be noted that what will have to be admitted over the drawbridge at the moment of our joining the Communities, will be more than the law contained simply in the three treaties as such. We shall have to admit, at the same time, the whole range of subsidiary law which, upon the basis of the treaties, has been enacted by the Communities in accordance with their constitutions. This includes the 'general decisions', as they are called in the Coal and Steel Community, or the 'regulations' which is the name by which similar subsidiary laws are known in either Euratom or the Economic Community. All these, to the date of British entry into the Communities, must be admitted over the drawbridge at the same time as the Treaties themselves. In practice complex, the admission is in principle simple enough; it can be done by statutory enactment.

But the law of the Communities is not static. As those sectors of the national life of each member State, which are put into community by adherence to the treaties, are further and progressively integrated – which is, of course, the object of the exercise – so must the subsidiary laws and rules which give juridical expression to that integration make their way into the body of national law of each member State. In the vivid image of the President of the Court of Justice of the European Communities:* 'On the compact body of the internal legal orders, a collection of rules is grafted which is continually expanding in scope as integration develops and prospers. Just as the pathological multiplication of cells destroys living bodies by strangling their physiological functions, the growth of law-making by the extra-national authorities will, in the areas in which it operates, paralyse and ultimately annihilate the national legal orders, which will find themselves replaced by a new system better related to the aims being pursued.'

What is novel for the British constitution is not the lowering of the drawbridge to admit treaty law, principal or subsidiary, once made, to take effect alongside the existing law of the country. The novelty lies in the making of provision in advance for the unquestioning admission of subsidiary laws not yet made, at such time as they are made. For to admit them unquestioned is an obligation under the treaties; Parliament will not be called upon to fulfil its usual role. As if by a wave of the wand, the moat and drawbridge will have disappeared, as far as the subsequent subsidiary laws of the Communities are concerned. It is in this respect

*In his Foreword to *The Court of Justice of the European Communities; Jurisdiction and Procedure* by the present author, Butterworths, 1966, p. XIII.

that many people, with justification, point to the surrender of parliamentary sovereignty.

Parliamentary sovereignty, however, as has been shown earlier, is not identical or co-terminous with state sovereignty. It is by an act of state sovereignty that the United Kingdom would adhere to the treaties, and the inevitable consequence of that act is that parliamentary sovereignty would cease to be exercised in the usual way in respect of subsidiary laws of the Communities made after adherence. But it is hardly a quibble to suggest – because such is the fact – that state sovereignty itself would be not so much surrendered as pooled. For the United Kingdom, through its membership of the Communities' Council of Ministers, would have a part, together with the ministerial representatives of all other member States, in the making of the subsidiary laws which are to be automatically admitted to join the internal body of United Kingdom law. At the same time, the United Kingdom would join with the ministerial representatives of all the member States in making the laws which would be automatically admitted to the respective internal legal systems of each of the *other* member States. The fact that the Council of Ministers owes a primary duty to the Communities does not convert a pooling of sovereignty into surrender of it.

Parallel to the positive law-making, subsidiary to the treaties, that is bound to continue in the Communities as the process of integration develops, and which is the responsibility of the executive–administrative institutions, there is evolving the body of case law made by the Communities' Court of Justice in interpretation and application of the treaties and their subsidiary laws. This case law would, if the United Kingdom joined the Communities, be just as authoritative for the courts of this country, as the community treaties and subsidiary laws themselves are binding. At the moment of British adherence, it would be obligatory for the body of community case law, as it then stood, to be deemed forthwith to be authoritative in the United Kingdom. From that moment on, decisions of the Communities' Court of Justice in particular cases would similarly be of automatic effect – so far as they were applicable – in respect of parties within this country, or, it might be, in respect of the State itself.

But here again, it is not a matter of surrendering British judicial sovereignty to a totally alien body, because there would be British participation in the judicial work of the Communities' Court, whose decisions are just as binding – where applicable – on and in all other member States as on and in the United Kingdom. Rather is it a matter of the pooling of judicial sovereignty.

Seen from the mainly constitutional point of view of their impact within the United Kingdom, the judgments of the Communities' Court made after the British adherence would fall into two broad categories.

There is the type of judgment which, though given in a case brought, it may be, by some particular person(s) or industrial undertaking(s), is in fact declaratory of law applicable generally to all within the jurisdiction of the Communities. This is always true of a judgment that some administrative or legislative measure of one of the community institutions is not legally valid and is therefore pronounced to be quashed. Such a judgment, as the Latin expression favoured by the Continentals puts it, takes effect *erga omnes*, that is, not only in respect of those persons or undertakings that applied to the court to secure that result, but of everybody else in the Community as well. But, apart from this particular example, many judgments which are not concerned with the questioning of some measure or other, do in fact declare community law in a general way, at least indirectly. What is the correct meaning of this or that article of a community treaty? Does it directly confer rights on the nationals of member States without their parliaments taking any action in the matter? – and so on. Whoever may have applied to the court to find the answer to such a question, the answer may be of general interest and application. Of all judgments of this type, having general application, it will be necessary for British courts to take cognizance, even if no British subject had a hand in applying to the Communities' Court to obtain any one of them.

A second broad type of judgment of the Communities' Court is that which is directly applicable to a person (or an undertaking) subject to the jurisdiction of one of the member States. For example, the court may give judgment confirming that a fine or penalty is to be paid by such a person or undertaking. Thus, it might come about that a British industrial undertaking was ordered by the Communities' Court to pay a fine because of non-compliance with some Regulation made by the Commission or Council. A judgment of this type becomes enforceable in the United Kingdom, not by the Communities' Court itself, which has no means of compelling enforcement, but by the instrumentality of the British system for the administration of justice and its ordinary methods of civil procedure – for such enforcement by its national authorities is an obligation which any State undertakes on adhering to the treaties.

Such, in outline, are the ways in which adherence to the Communities would have an impact on British sovereignty – on parliamentary supremacy, on state sovereignty, on the body of United Kingdom law, and on certain aspects of the administration of law in this country by the Judiciary. It is an outline of constitutional principles only; it shows the channels and methods whereby certain modifications would be brought about in our traditional constitutional practices and in the body of positive law under which we live.

To attempt to review in full detail what the modifications in our positive law would in fact consist of would be to go far beyond the scope of this book. Suffice it here to say that in the British public generally there has probably been a greater tendency to exaggerate than to minimize the extent of those modifications. However that may be, the Communities do not, as has been shown, run counter to the basic elements of a free society; rather do they enhance them by internationalizing their field of application. Nor would any part of British criminal law, either its substance or its procedure, be subjected to change by the impact of our adherence to the Communities. Our law of contract and tort would not be basically affected, although certain particular contracts, restrictive of competition and free trade within the Communities, would be rendered invalid by community law. There would be no change in the constitutional position of the Queen, or in the allegiance owed by British subjects. It is rather in certain areas of our national law bearing on economic activity, such as taxation law, restrictive practices law, exchange control law, regulations relating to the free movement of labour, and such like, that the more obvious modifications will be brought about; patent law and perhaps company law may in course of time be modified; other areas of our ordinary law may also be pervaded to some extent by the influence of community law. But the Communities, as at present designed, have not been brought into existence with a mandate to unify, or even to harmonize, *all* the law of *all* the member States; they exist to promote economic unification and expansion, and it is essentially only on national laws that relate to these matters that their impact will be directly felt in this country. The essential and immediate concern of the Communities is with customs duties; agriculture; the free movement of labour, services and capital; transport; monopolies and restrictive practices; state aids for industry, and the regulation of the coal and steel, and nuclear, industries.

In future years the Communities may come to embrace wider issues within their active concern. For they were established, in the words of the Preamble of the E.E.C. Treaty, 'to establish the foundations of an ever closer union among the European people', extending, in the intention of the founders, to some form of political union. Progress along the road to that ultimate goal has been seriously impeded for the present (see Chapter 5) but between that goal and the present immediate concern of the Communities lies a wide-ranging series of aims conveniently summarized in the terms of Article 2 of the E.E.C. Treaty: 'to formulate throughout the Community a harmonious development of economic activities, a continuous and balanced expansion, an increased stability, an accelerated raising of the standard of living and closer relations between its member States'. The positive achievement of these aims may conceivably require the making of fresh laws applicable throughout the Communities, which, though not striking at the roots of the long established ordinary law of the member States, may exercise a modifying influence upon that law by conditioning the legal transactions that in fact could be validly made by virtue of it.

If the United Kingdom were to join the Communities the free exercise of her sovereignty in treaty relations with countries outside the Europe of the Six would be limited in the following ways. The freedom to negotiate commercial agreements would be subject to the principle that during the transitional period, before the common market is fully established (which, as far as can be judged at the time of writing, will be very soon), all negotiations with non-member States concerning the Community's external customs tariff are to be conducted by the European Commission (subject to supervision by the Council of Ministers, acting by unanimous vote during the first two stages of the transitional period, and by qualified majority vote for the remainder of it). When the transitional period is ended the European Commission will, *inter alia*, negotiate tariff or trade agreements with countries not members of the Communities (subject to supervision by the Council acting by qualified majority vote). (See E.E.C. Treaty, Articles 110–116 and 228.) Furthermore, within the framework of any international organization of an economic character (for example, O.E.C.D., the World Bank, the International Monetary Fund), member States of the Communities may only proceed, after the transitional period, in matters of particular interest to the Common Market, by way of common action, the scope and implementation of which are to be determined by the Council acting by means of a qualified majority. During the transitional period, however, the obligation of member States of E.E.C. is only (Article 116) to consult together with a view to concerting action and adopting as far as possible a uniform attitude. Again, though the E.E.C. Treaty provides (Article 234) that it shall not affect rights and obligations arising from prior agreements between a member State and a non-member, the member State is obliged to take all appropriate steps to eliminate any proven incompatibilities with the treaty of such a prior agreement. Finally, Article 224 of the E.E.C. Treaty provides:

Member States shall consult one another with a view to taking in common the necessary steps to prevent the operation of the Common Market from being affected by measures which a member State may be called upon to take in case of serious internal disturbances affecting law and order (*ordre public*), in case of war or serious international tension constituting a threat of war, or in order to carry out undertakings into which it has entered for the purpose of maintaining peace and international security.

BELGIUM

In Belgium, as in all the other countries except the United Kingdom with which this book is concerned, the law which safeguards individual liberties and the basic freedoms of life as they now exist is not the outcome, as in Britain, of a lengthy process of piecemeal development in which individuals, at particular moments of history, played the outstanding part. As elsewhere in continental Europe, such law is contained in a single constitutional document, set down at one particular moment of the country's history, when, as it were, the development of the nation's life was fleetingly arrested, in order that there might be established a firm and lasting constitutional base upon which it could march forward in certainty. For Belgium, the moment came in the 1830s, following revolution, breakaway from the Netherlands and the emergence of the Belgian nation. This was a moment of self recognition, of conscious assessment of the nation's personality, and its written definition in legal terms.

Only so far as a national personality, with all its enduring attributes and capacity for development, is capable of definition in constitutional terms, of being made the subject of a true legal portrait, can a written 'Constitution' be of lasting value – or perhaps even of thoroughly reliable legal validity, because if it is not in character it will inevitably be rent asunder. A living organism, a nation reflects and defines its personality in its 'organic law' – an expression which lawyers use as an alternative to 'constitutional law'.

As in other countries, it was a National Congress, elected by the people, that in Belgium made the original portrait. That was on 7 February 1831, and, with a few amendments, it applies today. (From 1814 until 1830 the country had been united with Holland. A provisional separate government for Belgium was set up at Brussels on 25 September 1830, and asked the people to elect their National Congress. Duly elected on 3 November, the Congress confirmed Belgium's independence on the 18th, and the Constitution was promulgated in the following February.

Meantime, on 2 December 1830, the principle of the independence of the State of Belgium had been recognized by the Conference of London, and later was guaranteed by the Treaty of London of 19 April 1839, signed by Austria, France, Great Britain, Prussia, the Netherlands and Russia.)

'All powers emanate from the people. They shall be exercised in the manner established by the Constitution', states Article 25 of the Constitution. A series of articles (4–24)* establishes the rights of Belgian citizens, and in some instances specifically speaks of these being guaranteed (for example, by Article 7, 'individual liberty is guaranteed'; so are religious liberty and the free expression of opinion in all matters). The ultimate constitutional guarantee lies in the oath taken by the Monarch on succession to the throne, to maintain the Constitution. In this way the rights of citizens which are upheld include: equality before the law, individual liberty, privacy of the domicile, due process of law, freedom from confiscation of property, religious freedom, freedom of the press, peaceful assembly, the right to petition public authorities, privacy of correspondence, linguistic freedom, the right to bring action against public officials, and the right to trial by jury in all criminal cases and for all political offences and offences of the press. Foreigners are granted protection of their personal property 'except as otherwise established by law', but 'full naturalization alone admits foreigners to equality with Belgians in the exercise of *political* rights'.

All this will mostly seem familiar ground to the British reader. And indeed it is. For some of it was inspired by the example of his own country, or by the example of France and its famous Declaration of the Rights of Man. It is all basic to the broad tradition and foundation of western democratic civilization. Some of the procedures, by which the individual may legally enforce his individual rights, may be different from those in the United Kingdom, but substantially the rights and freedoms are the same or closely similar.

Thus it is fitting that it was in Belgium that the earliest positive steps were taken, in the aftermath of the Second World War, for international collaboration on a European regional basis in the

*See Appendix 2.

defence and advancement of fundamental human rights and the values of western civilization. The Brussels Treaty Organization of 1948 has been sufficiently described in a preceding chapter. That was the first step. Belgium followed it with membership of the Council of Europe, the European Convention on Human Rights (ratified by it on 14 June 1955), O.E.E.C., and later O.E.C.D. Belgium joined the European Coal and Steel Community in 1952 (the story of the Belgian coal-mines constitutes one of the outstanding chapters in the history of that Community) and in 1958 the European Economic Community and Euratom. Belgium is thus as fully committed as any other country not merely to European unification by way of international collaboration, but to its unification by positive integration, economically (and politically), with the other countries of the Six.

There is no point in describing here the pooling with the other five member countries of the exercise of certain attributes of her sovereignty, that Belgium agreed to on ratifying the Community treaties. What has been said in the preceding chapter in respect of the United Kingdom, were she to join, applies equally, of course, to Belgium and to each of the other five member countries.

The procedure by which Belgium becomes a party to an international treaty bears a close resemblance to that of the United Kingdom: the Monarch 'makes treaties of peace, of alliance, and of commerce', though 'treaties of commerce, and treaties which may burden the state, or bind Belgians individually, shall take effect only after having received the approval of the two houses' (i.e. the House of Representatives and the Senate – Article 68 of the Constitution). It was with that approval that Belgium ratified each of the three treaties setting up the European Communities, of which she thus became an original member. The Belgian 'drawbridge' was lowered and the treaties were admitted to form part of the body of Belgian law.

But there the similarity stops. For the Belgian constitution gives the Parliament no power to convert an international treaty into an internal 'Statute'. The procedure by which the treaty provisions are made fully operative inside Belgium has therefore to be something like the reverse of what happens in Britain; instead of Parliament taking over the treaty, as it were, from the treaty-making power (the Queen with her Ministers) which entered into it, and converting it to internal use, the Belgian Parliament needs to delegate to the King who entered into the treaty an increase in executive power, in order that this may be used to give internal effect in Belgium to the Community treaties – and to subsidiary law made by the Communities by virtue of the treaties.

In this way, for example, a law was enacted by Parliament on 2 May 1958 delegating to the King the power to implement decisions of the European Economic Community modifying customs duties, and in consequence Royal Decrees could be made on 17 December 1958, 7 December 1960, and 27 December 1960 (and ministerial orders on 18 December 1959, and 14 December 1960) relating to the application of the E.E.C. Treaty. Similarly, a law of 14 July 1959 gave the King the right to take the necessary measures for the production, distribution, purchase, sale and transport of solid mineral fuels, and on that basis Royal Decrees were made on 30 December 1959 (and ministerial orders on 26 and 28 January 1960) in order to give effect within Belgium to a decision (45/69) of the High Authority of the European Coal and Steel Community. An example of this procedure in operation over a more general area, is that of the Royal Decree of 26 July 1962 providing for the implementation by the executive of the European Economic Community's agricultural measures.

But all these decrees and orders were required to be submitted to the two Houses of Parliament for approval during the year following their entry into force (the Royal Decree of 17 December 1958 mentioned above, for example, was given approval by a law of 27 June 1960). In fact, there has not so far been any difficulty about obtaining the requisite approval, though by the time it was passed into law the decrees and orders to which it related had sometimes fulfilled their purpose, and lapsed. Unless there is to be disapproval on some occasion, this procedure for approval may come to appear merely perfunctory. But the possibility of disapproval may be deemed an important safeguard of basic freedoms in Belgium, though from the Community point of view it would seem to be potentially a drag on the harmonious application in all member countries of community law. Community decisions addressed individually to Belgian individuals or corporate bodies (such as industrial undertakings), whether these decisions are made by a Community executive institution or are judgments of the Communities' Court of Justice, are made enforceable in Belgium by procedures prescribed in a law of 2 May 1957 (respecting the Coal and Steel Community) and in a draft law (respecting the other two Communities as well) introduced in the House of Representatives on 13 July 1966.

Like all other Western European countries Belgium has experienced an intensification of the intervention of government in the day-to-day affairs of the people. Belgian citizens have, however, long been familiar with a system whereby they could defend their rights and liberties against unlawful encroachment of administrative power exercised by the public authority. Where such intervention could be demonstrated to be unlawful, her citizens could find their protection in the ordinary courts of the land (until 1946, when lawsuits of this kind were made triable by a special administrative court, called, like the French body it was created to resemble, the 'Conseil d'État'). And, for this, their constitution provided the firm basis that 'no authorization is necessary to bring action against public officials for the acts of their administration, except as provided for ministers' (Article 24). Consonantly with the public interest, individual liberty was legally safeguarded, and the specific methods and procedures by which this was made possible had been brought to a highly developed system (since 1831 by the ordinary courts and after 1946 by the Conseil d'État) by the time Belgium came to adhere to the European Coal and Steel Community Treaty in 1951. Very similar principles of administrative law to those to which Belgians had thus become accustomed were embodied in the Coal and Steel Treaty, and in the two later treaties setting up the Economic Community and Euratom. Their purpose, in the treaties, was to give protection to individuals and corporate bodies, in Belgium as in the other five member countries – as well as to the six States themselves – against administrative action by the Communities' executive institutions which could be shown to be unlawful by the terms of the treaties themselves, or by the terms of subsidiary legislation made by virtue of the treaties.

So the Belgian laws of 2 May 1957 and 13 July 1966, making enforceable in Belgium the community decisions addressed individually to her citizens or corporate bodies, were confronted by the corollary, familiar to Belgium, of protection by court proceedings – though now on a community and not on a national plane – against any such decisions not thoroughly lawful in terms of community law. The details of this protection on the community plane, which are really a matter of the 'constitutions' of the Communities, must, however, be deferred to Chapter 4. Here it need only be said that successful recourse to this protection will of course prevent the implementation internally in Belgium of the community administrative or legislative measures against which it is sought.

To return, then, to the main methods by which community law is implemented internally in Belgium. It can readily be appreciated that the fact that these are not the same as those used in other countries of the Six (or those that would presumably be used in the United Kingdom) means a potential lack of uniformity in the application of community law over the whole of the geographical territory covered by the Communities. From the point of view of the Communities, of course, such uniformity is more than a desirable goal – the extent to which it is complete is a very measure of success in effectively establishing the Communities themselves.

But probably a greater problem for the Communities than any lack of uniformity that may result from the different methods used in the respective member States for giving internal effect to community law has been, and still is, the varying legal positions in the member States regarding the relationship between the ordinary internal law of the country and community law having internal effect. Does this latter take precedence over the former? Is it, to use the favourite continental expression, paramount? Though the Community treaties indicate, either indirectly or by implication, an intention that community law should be treated as paramount over the ordinary law in each member State, they contain no express provision to that effect. (It has frequently been suggested that when, as is contemplated, the three treaties are merged into one, the opportunity should be taken of incorporating such an express provision.) For the present, therefore, this question is in practice largely dependent on the constitutional law of each member State.

The question sub-divides in fact into two parts, which, without delving immediately into the abstruse legal theories with which they are concerned, may perhaps be fairly described as follows:

First, it must be determined whether community law takes precedence not only over internal law as it stands at the moment of community law coming into force, but also whether it does so in such a way that no subsequently enacted internal law can have any effect contrary to community law. Some indication of the likely answer in the United Kingdom to this part of the question was given in the preceding section. The second part of the question concerns the relationship between community law and, not the *ordinary* internal law of a member State, but its *constitutional* law. In some countries of the Six, notably Italy and Germany, there has been a tendency for the courts, confronted with an element of community law in a domestic case on which they were called upon to decide, to doubt the internal *constitutionality* of some aspect of community law, though not its internal enforceability on any other ground.

How does this matter stand in Belgium? The Belgian constitution – its national legal portrait – was made somewhat early. In 1831 and for some years thereafter statesmen and lawyers were hardly ever confronted with the task of giving internal effect, in detail, to obligations assumed by international treaty. The Belgian constitution did not therefore contain any provision as to the relationship between international and internal law. The expedient of regarding community law for the purposes of the present question as no different, in principle, from international law (as has been done in other member States of the Six whose constitutions define the relationship of international to internal law) and find the required answer in that way, was consequently not an expedient that could be used in Belgium.

A revision of the constitution (Article 68) is, however, contemplated, and this would have the effect of establishing the paramountcy of international (and community) law over internal law. In the meantime, part of the answer has been provided by the reliance by other courts on a decision of the Supreme Court of Appeal (Cour de Cassation) of 1925 that an international treaty approved by the legislative assembly, and entering into force after an internal law, arrests if need be the effects of that law. (That case was concerned with the effect of the Treaty of Versailles, on the conclusion of the First World War, and an earlier Belgian decree-law.)

But there are as yet no provisions in the Belgian constitution which explicitly or implicitly prohibit the legislature from passing a law at variance with an international treaty concluded at an earlier date. In 1953, a proposal was made to the Special Committee of the House of Representatives that was then dealing with constitutional revision, to amend Article 107 by a provision debarring the courts from applying domestic laws that are at variance with international treaties. The suggestion was rejected at that time because it would have placed the courts in a role thought to be properly reserved to the legislative and executive authorities. In 1959, an amendment concerning Article 68 was rejected, though on different grounds; it was felt advisable to wait for greater uniformity, among States generally, with regard to the relationship between international and internal law. At the time of writing (summer 1968) this part of the question is again under active consideration in Belgium.

The second part of the question – the possibility of community law being declared unconstitutional within the State – does not arise in Belgium, because of the nature of the constitution. An international treaty cannot be challenged by either the courts or the Legislature.

FRANCE

In the attainment of individual liberties and fundamental freedoms it would be difficult to imagine a route more different from the British than that followed to a very similar conclusion by the great nation whose motto was once more proclaimed in its recent constitution of 1958 to be 'Liberty, Equality, Fraternity'. From the overthrow of the Monarchy after 1789, through all the oscillations that followed between parliamentary and republican forms of government, on the one hand, and the caesarism of more personal rule, on the other – through Republic, Consulate, Empire, Restoration, Republic again, Empire again, Republic a third time in the 1870s, a fourth time in 1946, and a fifth in 1958 – one all-resistant motif has been 'the Rights of Man and the principle of the sovereignty of the nation as defined by the Declaration of 1789'. It is to these, reaffirmed and complemented in the Republican constitution of 1946, that again, in the Preamble to that of 1958, 'the French people . . . solemnly proclaims its attachment'.

Perhaps more hot-blooded than the British, but no less defiant, it was rather by the groundswell of popular sentiment than the dogged determination of individuals that the French, nearly two hundred years ago, arrived where the British had come somewhat earlier. And they did so, perhaps, with a greater national awareness of what they were positively out to achieve. Theirs was a goal, they felt, that could be lastingly defined in a single document, theirs was a national personality of which the legal attributes should be portrayed in a portrait of permanent veracity and likeness. In this, their difficulty, which even now perhaps they may not finally have solved, was to make a legal portrait adequately reflecting all the manifold versatility of the national genius. But at the root of all lay the Rights of Man – to these, in spite of all the constitutional oscillations of the nineteenth and twentieth centuries, and even the threat to which enemy occupation in the Second World War exposed them, there is an unwavering national attachment which has been the inspiration of many other countries both on the Continent and overseas.

This was the nation which, after a century of feud and war with her age-old enemy Germany, and finally, occupation and attrition at her hands, rose, in the words of Sir Winston Churchill, in the early 1950s, to take Germany by the hand and lead her back into the family of nations. This was the act which, probably more than any other, secured the basis for the new Europeanism which was dawning over the ravaged continent at that time. That was in 1950–51, and the act took the form of France joining with Germany as the prime movers in setting up the European Coal and Steel Community.

But before that France was already at work in the Brussels Treaty Organization, in the Council of Europe, in O.E.E.C. then later in Western European Union and O.E.C.D., all of which have been described in outline in an earlier chapter. It is true that Western European Union owed its origins, as an extension of the Brussels Treaty Organization, to the rejection by the French Parliament in August 1954 of the Treaty for the European Defence Community (the 'European Army'), of which the legal design owed so much, as had the Coal and Steel Community, to French inventive genius. Another quirk, or stroke of irony, was that France, the land of the Rights of Man, has not ratified the European Convention of Human Rights – though perhaps French logic would maintain that for France to do so would be superfluous. It is also true – though these are essentially political matters strictly outside the scope of this book – that France lost interest in the North Atlantic Treaty Organization, under the protective shield of which so much of European achievement in the 1950s and early 1960s had been possible, and that in her recent phase of relative caesarism she has displayed a somewhat over-selfish attitude in respect of the European Communities.

Nevertheless, it is mainly to French legal and economic inventiveness that the creation of the European Communities is due, and without which they would probably never have seen the light of day. Apart from the overall novelty of the community system, when it was introduced in 1951, there was also one particular element in it which was frankly transplanted, as it were, from the French national *milieu* to that of the Coal and Steel Community. That element was the system of administrative law embodied in the treaty to guarantee to all parties, member States, individuals, and industrial undertakings alike, that enforceable legal controls should ensure that the High Authority – the very powerful, independent, central executive authority of the Community – should not with impunity exceed its powers. Indeed, the very technical legal terms with which administrative law is defined within France internally, were, to the satisfaction of all the other member States, embodied virtually unchanged in the Community Treaty – though, of course, they have to be interpreted there in a community sense, and not merely against the background of their

French legal origin* or that of administrative law as practised internally in the other member countries. So here France was on familiar ground; her internal system of administrative law, which, probably more than any other existing system in the world, protects the interests of the citizen against those of the State, even with the interventionist methods of government that are today familiar in the western democracies – that system was reproduced, as near as could be, in the Communities.

But, before proceeding to investigate further the general legal effect on France of joining the Communities it would be as well at this point to take a look for a moment at the nature of the general body of law that applies within the territory of France (and of her Overseas Territories) and then at the way the constitution protects it from undesired incursions of law from outside.

Until the Napoleonic codification of the early nineteenth century (producing the Civil Code, the Code of Civil Procedure, the Commercial Code, and also the Criminal Code and the Code of Criminal Procedure) private law in France was to be found almost only in custom based largely on the precepts of Roman law. (Custom was also of the greatest importance in other branches of French law.) Legislation, until that time, had only very infrequently been concerned with private law. (There had been, for example, ordinances in 1667 on civil procedure, in 1673 on commerce on land, in 1681 on merchant marine and maritime commerce, in 1731 on donations, in 1735 on wills; and some of these ordinances made changes in the customary law.)

From the early nineteenth century onwards 'enacted law' has replaced custom as the primary source of all French law, including private law. Enacted law (referred to by the generic expression 'La Loi') may, however, be the result either of express enactment by the *Legislature* (and thus resemble in kind a Statute enacted by the British Parliament) or of legal provision of a general and permanent nature, made by the Executive (in exercise of what is called its 'pouvoir réglementaire' – its 'regulatory power').

When enacted law is of the former kind, being what the British lawyer would look upon as a Statute proper, it is technically

*Of which a brief account was given in Chapter 2.

known as 'une loi'. In the hierarchy of French sources of law, the 'loi' (or statute) stands supreme; the great Codes, to which reference has just been made, stand no higher, for in essence they are themselves 'lois' being called codes simply because they deal with a broad area of law and not some particular segment of it as is the case with most other 'lois'. (It should here be stressed that French administrative law, which forms a very important part of the whole, is not codified and consists primarily in the judicial decisions of the Conseil d'État.) When enacted law is of the second kind – a legal provision of a general and permanent nature issuing from the Executive, and made by virtue of its 'pouvoir réglementaire' – it is known as a 'décret'. A 'décret' may not contain provisions contrary to those of une loi. Similarly, next lower down the hierarchy, an 'arrêté' (like a 'décret' but made by an individual Minister or by a head of local government such as a Préfet) must not conflict with any 'décret'.

[So-called decree-laws (décrets-lois) having the force of 'Statute' (loi) could formerly be made by the Government, if in times of emergency or in exceptional conditions the Legislature had granted special powers to the Government for that purpose. Such decree-laws might modify existing statutes or introduce, with statutory force, legislation that was entirely new. The constitution of 1946 (Article 13) aimed to prevent this undesirable practice which might virtually vest the whole legislative power in the Executive by delegation. The constitution of 1958 (Article 38) provided instead for ordinances (ordonnances): 'The Government may, for the execution of its programme, request Parliament to authorize it to take by ordinances, for a limited period, measures that are normally within the domain of law' (that is to say, outside the 'pouvoir réglementaire'). 'Ordinances shall be passed by the Council of Ministers following consultation with the Conseil d'État. They shall enter into force upon publication but shall become null and void if the Bill for their ratification is not submitted to Parliament before the date set by the Enabling Act. At the expiration of the time limit referred to in the first paragraph of this article the ordinances may be modified only by law in those matters which are within the legislative domain.']

Custom remains a source of French law, but now occupies a

secondary position and fulfils in practice a somewhat limited role. Judicial decisions, though they do not constitute binding precedents as in the English system, have a considerable persuasive force, particularly when given by the highest courts. In practice, all judicial decisions tend to base themselves expressly on the text of some article in the codes or statutes, as part of the reasoning (motivation), leading to the decision, which the law requires.

What is the impact of treaties on the body of law thus constituted? 'The President of the Republic shall negotiate and ratify treaties', states Article 52 of the 1958 Constitution. The same article also requires, in respect of international agreements (such as those that are inter-governmental rather than inter-State and so are not graced with the name of 'Treaty') that the President 'shall be informed of all negotiations leading to the conclusion of an international agreement not subject to ratification.' Moreover,

peace treaties, commercial treaties, treaties or agreements relative to international organization, those that imply a commitment for the finances of the State, those that modify provisions of a legislative nature, those relative to the status of persons, those that call for the cession or addition of territory, may be ratified or approved only by a law. They shall take effect only after having been ratified or approved

states Article 53. And it must be borne in mind that by requiring 'ratification or approval only by a law' the ultimate protection of the body of internal law from treaty influence is placed fairly and squarely in the hands of Parliament, since Article 34 provides: 'All laws shall be passed by Parliament.' The French Parliament thus enters into the treaty-making process somewhat more completely than does that of the United Kingdom, so that the image of moat and drawbridge which in that case was accurate (Chapter 2) had perhaps better be replaced here by an image of the sovereign people of France manning the outermost fortifications. For 'National sovereignty', states Article 3,

belongs to the people, which shall exercise this sovereignty through its representatives and by means of referendums. No section of the people, nor any individual, may attribute to themselves or himself the exercise thereof.

So much for the protection of the internal body of general law. But there is also the law of the constitution to be protected. 'The President of the Republic shall ensure that the Constitution is respected. He shall ensure, by his arbitration, the regular functioning of the governmental authorities, as well as the continuity of the State', provides Article 5. Here are duties that are equally incumbent on the President when he is negotiating treaties, as when he is concerned with any other aspect of affairs of State. Moreover, as will be shown in a moment, if 'an international commitment contains a clause contrary to the constitution' then the constitution itself must first be amended before the authorization to ratify or approve the commitment may be given. (Amendment of the constitution must be passed in identical terms by the two Houses of Parliament, and does not become final until approved by a referendum – Article 89.)

France has duly ratified the three community treaties, and it goes without saying that, like the other member States, she shares equally in the pooling of certain functions of State sovereignty that the Communities necessitate. But how does she stand in respect of the important question of the paramountcy of community law over internal law – of which question an outline has already been given in the preceding section dealing with Belgium?

The French constitution of 4 October 1958 (making, in this respect, no fundamental change from the constitution of 1946) provides, in Article 55:

Treaties or agreements duly ratified or approved shall, upon their publication, have an authority superior to that of ordinary legislation [*les lois*], subject, for each agreement or treaty, to its application by the other party.

Article 54 lays down that a treaty or agreement cannot be duly ratified or approved, if the Constitutional Council declares that it contains a clause that is at variance with the constitution, until the constitution has been revised. The three Community treaties have of course been duly ratified, and there is no doubt of their paramountcy over laws existing at the time of ratification.

But there has been some difference of opinion in France as to the exact legal status of a subsequent internal law running counter to the treaties. Admitting that the articles of the constitution just referred to should prohibit the Legislature from enacting such a conflicting law, what is the result if nevertheless this is done through inadvertence? Must a court, in such circumstances, refuse to apply the inconsistent law, upholding the treaty and in effect censuring the Legislature? Some body of opinion says no, but the courts of appeal have leaned against this opinion, since they consider it to be in disregard of the constitution. If this attitude is confirmed by a consistent case law of the courts, then, in France, the paramountcy of community law over both existing and subsequent internal legislation is established without question.

The second part of the question, that is, whether community subsidiary legislation can be tested for its internal constitutionality, may seem unlikely to arise in France. The provisions of the treaties, and the regulations made under them, that are directly applicable to the member States, are, in France, adopted where necessary to internal law by the use of the 'pouvoir réglementaire'. This power is vested by the 1958 constitution (Articles 9, 13, 19, 21 and 22) either in the President of the Republic, as Head of State, or in the Prime Minister, as head of government. When a community directive is addressed to France (a directive is the means by which the Community requires a specified objective to be attained but leaves it to the government of the member State concerned to determine the internal method by which this is to be done) – when this happens, and no internal legislation is necessary in consequence, the directive is given effect to in France by decree of the President or Prime Minister. Where, on the other hand, the directive does require internal legislation, the Government, on the basis of Article 38 of the constitution, may ask Parliament, in the way already mentioned, to 'authorize it, over a limited period, to take, by way of ordinances, measures normally the subject of legislation'.

Parliament's first law giving such an authorization was that of 14 December 1964 (no. 64–1231), the validity of which has been subsequently (6 July 1966) extended to 1 January 1970. The explanatory statement prefacing this law, when it was first introduced into Parliament in the form of a Bill, is revealing: 'Parliament has already accepted all the consequences flowing from the E.E.C. Treaty, including all the domestic legal measures it would necessitate, so that there appears to be no need for it to study all the implementing measures in detail. As regards the right of establishment and freedom to supply services, France's obligations have already been defined by two general programmes and by a very detailed liberalization timetable, which Parliament cannot tamper with without neglecting our international obligations.'

Finally, decisions – that is, the third method by which the Community may attain its objectives – are now, if addressed to France as a member State, given effect to by presidential decree. Decisions directed to individuals or corporate bodies within the jurisdiction of France are, under general decrees, made ultimately enforceable by order of the President of the Republic.

To sum up, France has gone a long way in the direction of unimpeded enforceability, within her territory, for community treaty provisions, regulations, directives and decisions. But Parliament has not altogether let go of the reins, since some of the authorization it has given (under Article 38 of the Constitution) must sooner or later come up for renewal.

THE GERMAN FEDERAL REPUBLIC

The well-known saying of Thomas Gray, 'Law is what the courts decide', was profoundly true of Britain at the time he said it, in the eighteenth century. As has been indicated, it would be far less true of that country today. But of continental European countries, and of Germany in particular, it would at no time have been true. In Germany law is what is prescribed by the legislator and by general custom.

Until barely a hundred years ago, Germany had not begun to establish her political identity as a nation. Consequently, legislator and general custom were not, until the late nineteenth century, anything like single forces contributing each on their own account to the growth and development of a unified body of general law applicable over the country as a whole – and even in the late nineteenth century the lack of strength of these two unifying forces can be gauged from the fact that it was not until 1900 that the general Civil Code (Das Bürgerliche Gesetzbuch) came into force. It is not possible, therefore, to conjure up a mental picture of German law either as the slowly evolved 'corpus' resulting from individual court judgments, and the stands made by individuals for their freedom at certain moments of history, which is true of Britain, or as the result, at least as far as their constitutional law was concerned, of what has been referred to earlier as the groundswell of popular sentiment, as it was in France. Rather must an image of German law be formed agains the impersonal and segmented background of Germany's political history.

The law of the Anglo-Saxons, the prelude to all English law, was indeed Germanic, and was of one kind with early German laws. But there was a parting of the ways, because in Germany there was no equivalent to the centralizing force that developed in Britain from the early English kings onward. Germany consequently developed local customs, not a generalized national system of law. In spite of the efforts of scholars, particularly from the early nineteenth century, to promote an overall uniformity, it could make little headway against the political trend. This, with some interruptions, was consistently in the opposite direction. As late as 1871 the 'Germany' that went to war with France and defeated her was not a unified Germany. It was a conglomeration of lesser states and principalities under the leadership of Prussia – and the war is appropriately known as the Franco-Prussian war. Only after that, with the setting up of the German Empire (Das deutsche Reich) in 1871, was there a political framework in which little by little it became possible to reverse the earlier centrifugal trend – expressed in what was virtually a legal axiom: 'City or local law prevails over provincial law, and provincial law prevails over general common law' ('Stadtrecht bricht Landrecht, Landrecht bricht Gemeines Recht').

The story of individual human rights must also be seen, like the rest of German law, against the background of the political history of a large number of individual States and principalities.

For it is in the respective constitutional laws of each of these, and in their attempts at codification of their general law from the eighteenth century onward, that human rights find their only expression. And although the general law was progressively unified after 1871 throughout the German Empire, the individual states retained their control of constitutional law, and of administrative law which was ancillary to it.

The German Empire was in fact a federated state, though it had many strongly centralized features. There was a Reich Government and a Reich Parliament (Reichstag) but each of the individual states had, besides its own King, Grand Duke, or Duke, both a government and a parliament. However, neither in the Reich nor in the individual states were the Governments responsible to the Parliament. The legislative power of the Reich was exercised by the Federal Council (Bundesrat), which was made up of all the Kings, Grand Dukes and Dukes or their deputies, acting together with the Reichstag – a house of representatives elected from the entire Reich.

The process of centralization was pursued further after the First World War with the establishment in 1919 of the Weimar Republic, on the basis of a democratic constitution (Die Weimarer Reichsverfassung). The States were converted into provinces (Länder), some of the smaller territories being merged into larger ones for the purpose, and the Reich, having been given wider powers of taxation, became consequently possessed of greater legislative power in relation to that of the Länder. It was now the Reichstag – an elected assembly formed by democratic representation – which exercised legislative power. For though the Reichsrat, representing the federated Länder, could object to a bill, the objection could be overridden by a two-thirds majority of the Reichstag or, in certain cases, by referendum. Though the Government of the Republic was made responsible to the Reichstag, it was appointed by the President of the Republic. The Länder retained considerable powers of administration, and a measure of legislative power. Weimar Germany became a member of the League of Nations in 1926, only to withdraw from it in 1932. It was the first nation to sign the Pact of Paris of 1928 renouncing war as an instrument of national policy, but from 1938 onwards it was conspicuous in violations of the pledge contained in that treaty.

Meantime, the 'National Socialist German Labour Party', which was originally formed in Munich as a small anti-semitic group strongly opposed to the social democratic and republican constitution of Weimar, finally came into power with Hitler as its leader when he became Chancellor in January 1933. When President Von Hindenburg died on 2 August 1934 and a plebiscite was subsequently held, Hitler received 88.1 per cent of the votes cast, which totalled about $43\frac{1}{2}$ million. From 1938 the sway of the 'Nazi' dictatorship over all rival elements was complete.

The Weimar Constitution was never expressly and completely revoked, but in the decrees issued by the dictatorship little regard was paid to it. The legislative activities of the Länder were gradually restricted, and the laws of the Reich were enacted, not by the Reichstag, but by the Reich government and later by Hitler ('Der Führer') himself. One of the principal purposes of all legislation during the period of dictatorship from 1933 to 1939 was to make the Nazi political ideology effective in every branch of the law. This could be done, and was, either by so-called 'amending' legislation affecting particular aspects of the existing law, or by completely fresh legislation in areas not previously touched by positive legislative provision.

But concurrently with the legislative process the judicial process was also turned to the same ideological purpose. In this, the fact that in Germany it was never at any time true that 'law is what the courts decide' – the fact that, unlike the common law of England, German law was not judge-made – meant that all that was necessary to achieve the ideological purposes of the dictatorship in the judicial realm was to ensure that a sufficient number of judges were sympathetic to the régime and that the discretion given to them in the application of the written law was gradually extended. Twenty or thirty years later, taking a historical view of this very sorry chapter in the annals of judicial institutions in Germany, German legal scholars point to the judicial sabotage of democracy, liberalism and socialism that occurred during the Weimar Republic. In Germany during that period there existed what was publicly referred to as a 'crisis of confidence' in the judiciary. A particular slant was given, for example, to the judgments of the Supreme Industrial Court (Reichsarbeitsgericht). There was abuse of the Criminal Code. Even the Supreme Court (Reichsgericht) (some of whose judges had publicly avowed their sympathy with Nazi tendencies long before 1933) did not stand aloof from this judicial sabotage – and not merely in the fairly frequent constitutional trials in which it was concerned. 'The result was,' states one German scholar,* 'that in those fields of law, which were of even the slightest political significance, a growing and finally nearly intolerable insecurity prevailed.' At the same time, 'the predominance of the state over the individual resulted in a gradual abolition of the spheres of freedom and protection granted in most modern states to the individual citizen.'†

If there was ever an object lesson showing the importance to a would-be democratic state of the independence of its Judiciary, this was it. But in the process of 'denazification' of German law after 1945, the fact that it had never been true that 'law is what the courts decide' made the implementation of Article 2 of Military Government Law No. 1 (30 August 1945) to that extent more straightforward:

Decisions of German courts and official agencies and officials, and legal writings supporting, expounding, or applying National Socialist objectives or doctrines shall not be referred to or followed as authority for the interpretation or application of German law . . .

For the purpose of the present study it is of no great importance to examine the rest of the process of 'denazification' of German law. It should, however, be mentioned that certain areas of law, such as for example the Civil Code of 1900, could re-emerge virtually unscathed from the Nazi period, and also that a considerable measure of continuity with pre-1933 methods of law formation is provided by the modern recognition, as formal

*Dr E. J. Cohn in *Manual of German Law*, London, H.M.S.O., 1950, Vol. I, p. 18.

†Ibid. p. 17; and see, in general, the revised new edition of this work (British Institute of International Law and Comparative Law and Oceana Publications, 1968), sections 41–5, pp. 27–30, with bibliographical and other references therein.

sources of law, only of enacted law (legislation) and of custom, and not of judicial decisions (though recent case law has in practice strong authority). What is important for the purposes of this book is to look at the new basis of constitutional law in Western Germany (the Federal Republic) and the steps which, on that basis, the country has taken in the movement towards European unification.

The Brussels Treaty of 1948, to which reference has been made in preceding chapters, expressed, *inter alia*, the resolution of the contracting States 'to take such steps as may be held necessary in the event of a renewal by Germany of a policy of aggression'. By the early 1950s, both the international situation and attitudes towards Germany had so far changed that the long term need was clearly recognized to bring Western Germany into the organization of the defence of Free Europe, on terms that both France and the United Kingdom could accept. As has been shown, this was in fact brought about in 1954 by the enlargement of the Brussels Treaty organization into Western European Union, with the inclusion of the Federal Republic of Germany, which ratified the 1954 agreement on 5 May 1955 (as well as of Italy, which ratified on 20 April 1955).

Meantime, on the 13 July 1950, the Federal Republic had acceded to the Statute of the Council of Europe. Even earlier, the three zones of Germany occupied by the United States, the United Kingdom and France, had, through the Commanders in Chief of these zones, ratified the Convention for European Economic Cooperation. When this was converted into the O.E.C.D. in 1960, the German Federal Republic adhered to the new convention in its own right. Long before, on 5 December 1952, it had ratified, in its own right, the European Convention on Human Rights.

That the Federal Republic was legally able, as early as 1950 and again in 1952 and 1960, to take such international action in its own right, was due to the fact that on 23 May 1949 it had been provided with a new constitution. This constitution, or Basic Law as it is usually called because of its German name of 'Grundgesetz', was promulgated against a general legal background which can be summarized as follows. With the signing on

7 May 1945 of formal surrender, the régime of Hitler had come to an end; the territory of the Reich had been placed under the four-power administration of the U.S.S.R., the United Kingdom, the United States, and France; no treaty provision was made for any future exercise of sovereign power by Germany as a nation, though it continued to be considered a 'state'.* When the political purposes of the U.S.S.R. showed a clear divergence from those of the other three war-time allies, a draft constitution was prepared for the German Länder included in the British, American and French zones. It was approved by the voters of these western zones of occupation in a general election held on 14 August 1949 and became the Grundgesetz. Over the same period, a constitution for the Russian zone of occupied Germany was prepared, and proclaimed at Berlin on 19 March 1949.

The Basic Law states that 'the Federal Republic of Germany is a democratic and social federal state' (Article 20) and that 'for the time being this basic law shall apply in the territory of the Länder of Baden, Bavaria, Bremen, Greater Berlin, Hamburg, Hesse, Lower Saxony, North Rhine-Westphalia, Rhineland-Palatinate, Schleswig-Holstein, and Wuerttemberg-Hohenzollern (Article 23); it also provides that 'it shall be put into force for other parts of Germany on their accession' (Article 23) and that it 'shall become invalid on the day when a Constitution adopted in a free decision by the German people comes into force' (Article 147).

It provides for international action to be taken by the Republic, as follows: 'The federation may, by legislation, transfer sovereign powers to international institutions' (Article 24); that 'in order to preserve peace the federation may join a system of mutual collective security' and that 'for the settlement of international disputes the federation will join the general comprehensive obligatory system of international arbitration' (Article 24); and that 'the general principles of international law shall form part of federal law' (Article 25). Activities tending to disturb peaceful relations between nations and 'especially preparing for aggressive war shall be unconstitutional' (Article 26).

The preceding two paragraphs, particularly the latter, show the basis on which Western Germany was able to participate in

*See *Rex v. Bottril ex parte Kuchenmeister* 1946 1 A.E.R. 635.

her own right in the above-mentioned international institutions, which were established in the 1950s. It was by the same token that the country became an original member of the European Coal and Steel Community in 1952, and of the Economic and Atomic Energy Communities in 1958.

But, better to understand the impact on law in the Federal Republic made by adherence to these various treaty arrangements, two further general factors concerning the internal legal situation of Western Germany need to be borne in mind.

The first of these factors is the full elaboration of basic human rights, constitutionally guaranteed in the internal law, that figures in Articles 1 to 19 of the Basic Law of 1949.*

The second is the fact that since Western Germany is a federal State, it is necessary to appreciate the respective responsibilities, for the internal law, of the Federal Government (and Constitution) on the one hand, and the Governments (and Constitutions) of the Länder, on the other. Legislative power of the Federal Government is vested in a bicameral body consisting of the Parliament (Bundestag) and the Federal Council (Bundesrat). Executive power is vested in the federal President, elected by a federal convention (Article 54); there is provision for a federal Chancellor (Article 63) elected by the Bundestag on proposal of the federal President. The 'Federal Government' consists of the federal Chancellor and the federal Ministers (Article 62). To the Federal Government falls the general supervision over the execution of the federal laws by the various Länder (Articles 83, 84, 85, and 86) and it has jurisdiction *exclusively* over foreign affairs, citizenship, freedom of movement, currency, customs, railways, posts and telecommunications, trademarks, federal employees, statistics and even cooperation with the states in criminal police matters and matters concerning the protection of the Constitution (Article 73). The Federal Government has jurisdiction *concurrently* with the Länder in matters of civil and criminal law, census, associations, sojourn and settlement of aliens, protection of works of art, matters relating to refugees, public welfare, citizenship of the Länder, war damages, war veterans, economy, workers' organizations, scientific research, expropriation, natural resources,

*Articles 1–19 of the Basic Law are printed in full in Appendix 5.

economic powers, agricultural land and leases, diseases, food, shipping and navigation, road traffic and non-federal railways (Article 74).

The Federation exercises judicial authority through the Supreme Federal Court (Bundesgerichtshof), the Federal Constitutional Court (Bundesverfassungsgericht) and through other federal courts established by the Constitution. There are, for example, the very important Federal Administrative Court (Bundesverwaltungsgericht), and also the Supreme Tax Court (Bundesfinanzhof) which reviews the decisions of the special administrative courts handling tax matters, (the Finanzgerichte), as well as the supreme court dealing by way of review with matters of social insurance (Bundessozialgericht) decided in the first instance by the social courts (Sozialgerichte).

The Länder exercise judicial authority through the courts of the Länder themselves. These comprise the ordinary courts dealing with civil and criminal matters, the ordinary appeal courts (Oberlandesgerichte), general administrative courts, special administrative courts, and even special courts for labour disputes (Arbeitsgerichte). There are courts of appeal in these last-named matters (Landesarbeitsgerichte); at the apex of this particular hierarchy stands the federal supreme court in labour matters (the Bundesarbeitsgericht).*

This, then, is in outline the body of law, and the system for the administration of justice in Germany, into which community law has to be incorporated. In spite of the complications which the federal system may seem to put in the path of smooth incorporation, this is almost certainly not as difficult as it might at first appear – partly because community law is almost exclusively concerned with economic and social matters, and does not require to be infiltrated into every branch of the internal law of any member State of the Communities. The process of the actual internal application of community decisions is also smoothed because of the comparative readiness with which German principles of administrative law can be assimilated to those of community law and vice versa (as can those of all six original member States). Moreover, in formulating the free competition and anti-

*See the table in Appendix 5.

monopoly provisions of the Rome Treaty for the European Economic Community the negotiators – avowedly – drew by far their greatest inspiration from the German internal (federal) law directed against restrictive practices (the Gesetz gegen Wett-bewerbeschränkungen, of 1957); like the French, who supplied much of the inspiration for the administrative law of the Communities, the Germans have similarly a particular area of community law in which they can perhaps feel specially at home.

But these are generalities. What of the actual procedure for the implementation of the community treaties, and the subsidiary legislation resulting from them, within Germany?

It has already been mentioned that 'the Federation may, by legislation, transfer sovereign powers to international institutions' (Basic Law, Article 24 (1)) and that 'the general rules of public international law are an integral part of federal law. They shall take precedence over the laws and shall directly create rights and duties for the inhabitants of the federal territory' (Basic Law, Article 25). The principle of the paramountcy of community law over the internal law of the Federal Republic would therefore seem to be unconditionally established by these constitutional provisions. But the question has been raised whether international treaties such as those establishing the European Communities do really constitute *general* rules of public international law. Moreover, Article 100 (2) of the Basic Law provides that: 'If in the course of litigation, doubt exists whether a rule of public international law is an integral part of federal law and whether such rule directly creates rights and duties for the individual (Article 25), the court shall obtain the decision of the Federal Constitutional Court'; so the further question is raised, whether the Basic Law in fact ensures with no more ado the paramountcy of the rules laid down by an international treaty over internal law since it also provides for the exercise of judicial control. German Länder courts have given different answers to these two questions.

A fundamental divergence became apparent in the closing months of 1963 in judgments given by two courts in different Länder. This divergence turned on the proper application to be made by these courts, in respect of regulations made by the

Council of E.E.C., of the principle of the separation of powers – legislative, executive and judicial – enshrined in the Basic Law. 'All state authority (of the Federal Republic) emanates from the people. It shall be exercised by the people in elections and plebiscites and by means of separate legislative, executive and judicial organs', states Article 20 (2). It is not only understandable but, indeed, highly desirable, that in the light of the very bitter experiences that had resulted from the slipping of legislative power in Germany in the 1930s into the hands of the Executive – a one-man Executive – that this cardinal provision of the new constitution of 1949 should be most jealously regarded and protected. If the Institution of E.E.C. responsible for Regulations was an executive body, then was it not unconstitutional for such Regulations to be implemented in the Federal Republic?

In referring to the German Federal Constitutional Court a dispute about agricultural duties (on malt barley) that was before it, the Financial Court of Rhine-Palatinate had, amongst other things, the following to say:

... the Federation may certainly transfer sovereign rights to international institutions by passing a law,* and accordingly transfer the right to make, by means of regulations, legal rules binding on all concerned throughout the Federation; but in doing so it must consider that the Basic Law prohibits any prejudice to the principle of the separation of powers; and the transfer of sovereign rights must not lead to the abrogation, from without, of the separation of powers which is carefully balanced and safeguarded by the Basic Law in order to preserve a free social order; the Basic Law is against authorizing executive institutions to issue regulations in amendment of the laws, but the authorization given under the (German) law† ratifying the E.E.C. treaty embodies regulations which amend the laws. ... Even if it is submitted that the E.E.C. Council creates a body of laws rather than a series of ordinances, the conclusion is inescapable that the (German) law ratifying the Community treaties violates the Basic Law and is thus unconstitutional. The principle of the separation of powers, which is essential to safeguard the free legal order established by the Basic Law, admits of exceptions contained in the Basic Law itself. In the sphere of legislation

*See the German law of 27 July 1957 relating to the two treaties signed in Rome on 25 March 1957 creating the E.E.C. and Euratom.
†Of 27 July 1957.

with which we are here concerned, the Basic Law allows the executive bodies to promulgate legal provisions of general binding force. But this can only be done if the Legislature grants the necessary authorization, the substance, purpose and scope of which it must determine, in the law [this is a reference to Article 80 (1) of the Basic Law; see appendix 5 – present author]. The Basic Law expressly deprecates any neglect by the Legislature of its responsibility to enact laws, by undue recourse to the delegation of its authority and by allowing the executive bodies to amend or make additions to laws, for example, by means of ordinances (Rechtsverordnungen) – or to issue such ordinances instead of laws.... The authors (of the Basic Law) thus made clear their intention as far as possible to restrict the legislative power vested in the Executive, for practical reasons. What is more they prohibit any derogation from the principle of the separation of powers. There is thus no doubt that the Federal Legislature would be violating the Basic Law if it allowed an executive authority to promulgate laws. The right of the Federal Legislature to be a party to international organizations finds an insurmountable limitation in the breach of a constitutional principle of cardinal importance.

In the opinion of the Financial Court of Rhineland-Palatinate there was a violation of the Basic Law resulting from an infringement of its Article 79 (3), whereby any amendment to the Law is to be deemed inadmissible if it affects the principles laid down in either Article 1 ('The basic rights shall bind the Legislature, the Executive and the Judiciary as directly enforceable law') or Article 20 ('Legislation shall be subject to the constitutional order; the Executive and the Judiciary shall be bound by the law').

To all this, the opposite view was taken by the Administrative Court of Frankfurt:

The Administrative Court does not agree with the opinion of the Financial Court of Rhineland-Palatinate that Article 1 of the law ratifying the E.E.C. Treaty is unconstitutional because, under Article 189 of the E.E.C. Treaty, the E.E.C. Council is empowered to issue regulations that are, for the Federal Republic also, binding in every respect and directly applicable.

The legislator was empowered to transfer to the E.E.C. sovereign rights relating to the direction and control of the national economy. He was empowered by the Basic Law to ratify the E.E.C. Treaty and in particular Article 189. Article 24 of the Basic Law authorized the

Federation to transfer sovereign powers and to consent to limitations of sovereignty, the former being further-reaching in its implications than the latter. The cession of sovereign powers through a treaty is only conceivable either as a due act of abdication, whereby the Federation, vested with these powers, once and for all, as a legal person, transferred its entitlement to their exercise and became consequently unable either in law or in fact to retract from such a transfer; or if the Federation, remaining as a legal person vested with these powers, transferred the right to their exercise. Since the authors of the constitution provided for two forms of transfer between which it deliberately made a distinction, it follows that the authorization provided for in Article 24 also applies to a permanent cessation of sovereign powers.

Similar or related constitutional questions lay at the root of a decision on 18 July 1967 by the German Supreme Financial Court (Bundesfinanzhof) to refer certain questions to the Communities' Court for a preliminary ruling and, pending its receipt, to adjourn the proceedings before it. These proceedings were on appeal from a refusal by the German Customs Office to release from payment of a 4 per cent turnover adjustment tax a firm which had in 1964 imported powdered milk from Belgium. The brunt of the argument put forward by the firm to the Supreme Financial Court rested on Articles 95 and 97 of the E.E.C. Treaty, alleging these were violated by the turnover adjustment tax rate – since it obviously discriminated against imports, because there was no turnover tax on domestic milk powder. Article 95 (1) of the treaty had been held by the Communities' Court in a decision of June 1966 to be immediately effective and to vest recognizable rights in individuals and private parties – without the necessity for any legislation of a member State to implement the Article – which the courts of member States were bound to uphold. Looking at the facts before it the Supreme Financial Court considered that to find in favour of the firm would be to admit as a general principle that a private party enjoyed a more extensive right to enforce the treaty than either the E.E.C. Commission, or member States – for they could only do so by directives or regulations and actions before the Communities' Court. Why should a private party be put in the position of being able to oblige his national courts to treat it as if the State to which it belonged had in fact fulfilled its treaty obligations, as it – and not necessarily the State – considered those obligations to be? In the questions that it formulated for a preliminary ruling of the Communities' Court, the Supreme Financial Court therefore asked the former to look again at its 1966 decision concerning Article 95 (1) of the treaty, and to decide specifically whether Article 95 can 'grant the right to private persons as a "self-executing rule" to demand, in proceedings before their national courts, to be treated, despite the provisions of the national law, as if the member State had already fulfilled its obligations under the Article to pass legislation, whereas by the text of the treaty a member State can only be obliged to fulfil its obligations by the Commission or by another member State'.

Setting this question against the background of German constitutional law the Supreme Financial Court stated, in another part of its judgment: 'The court has doubts about the decision of the Communities' Court that Article 95 is a

self-executing rule, that is, directly effective and vests recognizable rights in private persons which national courts are bound to respect. The court will confine itself to commenting on this one question, which is of especial importance for the constitutional structure of the Federal German Republic.... Article 20 (3) of the German Constitution obliges the Executive and Judiciary to observe the rules of law. In the sphere of revenue law the rules of law include, in addition to existing legislation, undisputed legal rules which contain generally valid legal principles, such as the constitutional principle of good faith, and (by virtue of express provisions of the constitution) the universally accepted principles of international law, which have precedence over legislation and create immediate rights and duties for persons within the Federal Republic's jurisdiction (Article 25 of the Constitution). But there is no equivalent provision for community law in the Constitution. Neither Article 24 of the Constitution (which is generally considered to be the legal basis of the Acts ratifying the E.E.C. and Euratom Treaties) nor the tax law in issue in the present case, provides that, or how far, community law has precedence over the law of the Federal Republic and creates direct rights and duties for private persons which the judiciary is bound to observe. The authoritative textbooks and the case law to date do generally assume that community law has precedence over German law. But there are some doubts about the extent of this precedence, because of the absence of any express rules on the matter, especially in cases where constitutional issues arise. It is possible to infer from the treaty, the Ratification Acts and Article 24 of the Constitution, the validity of legislative acts of the Community, that is, regulations issued by the Council and Commission, as a consequence of the transfer of sovereignty. In such cases community law takes the place of the individual States' laws by express positive legislation. Such community laws can also be applied by the Executive and the courts without special difficulties. It is a different matter when the treaty – granted that it takes precedence – obliges member States to abstain from certain courses of action in the interests of attaining the treaty's goals, that is, forbids the alteration of an existing legal situation, or demands the alteration of a legal situation contravening the treaty immediately or at a future date.

As more and more questions such as those put to it by the German Supreme Financial Court come to be ruled upon by the Communities' Court, so will the full meaning of 'Community' become progressively clarified. The case which has just been outlined throws into sharp relief the position of individuals and private parties in the Community. Although they are members of it by virtue of their being nationals of, or subject to the jurisdiction of, a State which is itself a member, their position as members of the Community, and the rights and duties deriving from that position, transcend their relationship to the member States. Furthermore, the membership and participation in the Community of individuals and private parties is direct, immediate. To be made effective it does not necessarily require a member State to mediate between private parties or individuals and community government. The extent of that direct participation, and more especially the extent of its automatic effectiveness, by the operation of no more than the treaty itself without any implementing legislation by either the Community or the member States, nevertheless need clarification.

Germany is not the only country to meet with constitutional problems in the reception of community law. Italy, as will be shown in the next section, has experienced comparable difficulties, and other countries have done so to less extent. In neither Germany nor Italy have the final answers been given,* and in the interplay of the work of the Communities' Court with that of the highest national courts it is to be expected that more complete and satisfactory solutions will be evolved.

With regard to the question of the application within the Federal Republic of community law (as distinct from the question of its paramountcy over German law), it must first be noted that in general the Federal Government avails itself of the procedures made available to it by Article 80 (1) of the Basic Law.† But the federal structure of Western Germany creates the special problem of the application of community law in the federated Länder. Article 70 (1) of the Basic Law provides: 'The Länder shall have the right of legislation in so far as this Basic Law does not confer legislative powers on the Federation.' But where a Community decision or directive falls neither within the exclusive competence of the Federation (Articles 71 and 73 of the Basic Law), nor within its concurrent legislative competence (Articles 72 and 74), it may well be asked whether the Federation's legislative bodies may, under the Constitution, enact implementing measures. This matter has been the subject of controversy. If the answer were no, it would be necessary, in order to give effect to the Community measures in question, for each Land Government to introduce its own law for the purpose.

This in turn would raise the question whether the Länder are bound by the decisions and directives of the Communities. It is, after all, the Federal Republic that is a member of the Communities, and Community decisions and directives are therefore addressed to it and not to the individual Länder. It was the Federation that signed the community treaties on the basis of Article 32 (1) of the Basic Law, which makes the maintenance of relations with foreign States its affair, and of Article 24 (1), which authorizes it to transfer sovereign rights to international institutions. Since the Federation had the right, under these constitutional provisions, to conclude the treaties, it would seem to

*A decision of the German Federal Constitutional Court of 18 October 1967 has already carried matters further. See footnote on p. 128.

†For the text of which, see Appendix 5, p. 212.

follow that the Länder of which it is composed are also bound by them, even though they are not individual members of the Community.

Some German authors even take the view that under the provisions of Article 32, and especially Article 24, the Federation must be able to give effect to community decisions, including those on matters that normally fall exclusively within the competence of the Länder. Opinions on this question are, however, sharply divided. But its practical importance is limited as most matters affected by community measures come within the exclusive or concurrent competence of the Federation.

In practice, the Federal Ministers and Bundesrat have agreed upon a workable compromise under which the Federation is entitled to take part, in the Councils of the Communities, in discussions falling within the competence of the Länder, on the understanding that the latter remain responsible for implementing – or, as it were, transforming – the decisions and directives arising in this way.

When the treaties were ratified the German legislators realized that implementing the treaties and other community provisions would involve many adjustments to internal laws. This is why the Law of Assent of 27 July 1957 stipulates in Article 2 that the Federal Government must notify the Bundestag and the Bundesrat before any decision is taken bringing into being provisions that are directly applicable, or necessitate the adoption of internal laws.

Within the Federal Republic the actual procedure of implementation of community law and subsidiary legislation varies as follows:

(a) *Directly applicable provisions of the treaties, and regulations.* In Germany a whole set of community *regulations* have been given effect to by laws. On the basis of these, the authorities have taken implementing decisions and issued administrative regulations. Such national provisions do not transform the community law embodied in the agricultural regulations, but either discharge the obligations imposed on the Federal Republic by these regulations or serve to bring domestic law into line with community law.

Moreover, the Government has in many cases been empowered by the Parliament to give effect, through regulations, to certain provisions of the treaties or decisions of community institutions. It should be noted that under Article 80 of the Basic Law the Government may only issue regulations if expressly authorized to do so by a law which determines the contents, purpose and scope of such authorization.

Thus, under Article 3 (1) of the law assenting to the Treaties of Rome, the Government is authorized to amend, by means of regulations issued with the Bundestag's approval, provisions relating to taxes (abgabenrechtliche Vorschriften) and in particular to the customs tariff. The tariff law of 14 June 1961 revoked the original authorization (by Article 88) but Article 77 of the same law granted a fresh authorization as regards the customs tariff. Under the terms of that article statutory orders issued by the government have to be notified to the Bundestag and Bundesrat. The Bundesrat may, within a period of four weeks, submit an opinion thereon to the Bundestag. Such orders have to be cancelled, if the Bundestag so demands, within four months of their publication. So far the Bundestag has never called for cancellation.

(b) *Directives.* In Germany, there is no general law for the delegation of powers in this sphere.

Directives are given effect to in the form of laws, statutory orders or administrative decrees (Verwaltungserlasse):

1. Where a law is necessary, the Federal Government generally introduces a draft law which may, depending on the matter concerned, also require the consent of the Bundesrat.

2. An order usually suffices where powers have been delegated for the issue of regulations for putting a directive into effect.

3. Administrative decrees suffice for applying a directive that does not involve amending a federal law or statutory order already in force.

German courts have already ruled on the legal effect of directives in the sphere of domestic law. Several courts have upheld the principle that directives are not directly applicable, but entail obligations only for States.

(c) *Decisions.* As to the effect of community *decisions* in the domestic legal system, the Fiscal Court of Rhineland-Pfalz, in a judgment delivered on 27 March 1963, upheld the view that an E.E.C. Commission decision addressed exclusively to the member States is not binding in any way on individuals. The court cited in support of this view the provisions of Article 189 (4) of the treaty. The same court confirmed this view in another decision on 25 March 1965. Community decisions therefore require to be put into effect by internal measures.

In the case of decisions *addressed to individuals*, as well as of judgments of the Court of Justice of the European Communities, the State has to intervene where these involve the enforcement of pecuniary obligations (Articles 192 of the E.E.C. Treaty, 164 of the Euratom Treaty and 92 of the E.C.S.C. Treaty). In Germany, according to the announcement of 25 August 1954, the Federal Minister of Justice is empowered to issue the order for enforcement of judgments of the Court of Justice and of decisions of the High Authority of the E.C.S.C. Through an announcement of 3 February 1961 this provision was extended to the institutions of the E.E.C. and Euratom.

ITALY

Italy, as the political entity we know today, is hardly more than a hundred years old. This is not the place to re-tell in detail the story of her unification; how such diverse elements as the kingdoms of Piedmont and of Naples, the Milanese-Venetian kingdom under the rule of Austria, the States of the Church governed by the Roman Pontiff, and the Duchies of Tuscany, Parma, Modena and Lucca became, together with Sicily and Sardinia, unified politically in a single state by the 1860s. To set the process of unification finally in motion had taken forty years or more from the time of the territorial dispositions made at the Congress of Vienna in 1815 (the settlement which for Italy was nothing of the kind). The achievement of unification was due to the revolutionary activity and patriotic ardour of the people, to the indefatigable republican propagandism of Mazzini, to the popular martial leadership of Garibaldi, and to the steadfast liberalism of the rulers of Piedmont-Sardinia, combined with the astute statecraft of their constitutional advisers, amongst whom Cavour stood out. Those are dry words to describe the seething turmoil of a whole nation seeking birth – or rather re-birth. They are dry words to portray all the intense manifestations of the human spirit which, in such variety and profusion, the process called forth.

One of those manifestations was the intellectual ferment that ran through the country. Before even the legislative reforms in France at the turn of the century, to which the Revolution had there given rise, Italian legal reformers, especially in Piedmont, Tuscany and Naples, were seeking to coordinate, unify, and bring up to date the heterogeneous law that prevailed. Privileges of cities or of guilds must be suppressed, circulation of goods and persons must be more free, agriculture promoted.

The numerous strands of Italian private law had been derived from such varied sources as the Roman Justinian (preponderant in all latin law), germanic law, ecclesiastical or 'canon' law, and the common law (customary, statutory, doctrinal or jurispruden-tial), and there was not the slightest difficulty in imposing upon this body of law the napoleonic codes which the conquering French army brought with it into Italy in the first decade of the nineteenth century. The preponderance of Roman law in the Italian system virtually ensured in any event that this could be done with ease. The existing Italian desire to modernize the law, and the almost inimitable simplicity of the French codes, together set the final seal on their acceptance in Italy. Even after 1815 the napoleonic codes survived in Lucca, whilst in many other Italian states the laws remained of predominantly French inspiration. It is true that in Lombardy and Venice the Austrian code of 1811 was applied, and that in Tuscany and the Papal States the napoleonic codes were abolished – without alternative new legis-lation being put in their place. Nevertheless, in matters of general law, as in most matters of general public concern, the Italians of the nineteenth century set their gaze on France.

Not all their leaders wished it to be that way. Mazzini wrote in a French review in 1835:

The *initiative* is lost in Europe, and while each of us ought to be working to recover it, we persist in trying to persuade the peoples that it still lives, active and potent. Since 1814 there has been a void in Europe, and, instead of labouring to fill it up, we deny the fact. From 1814 onwards, there has been no people to take the initiative, and yet we persist in saying the French people has the power to do so. *The French Revolution must be considered, not as a programme for the future, but as a summing up, not as the initiative of a new age, but as the formula closing an existing one.*

Thirty-six years later, as the final unification of Italy was at hand, he returned to this theme:

I see even to this day, more vivid and potent than I had believed, the inordinate prestige possessed by France and the memories of its great Revolution over the minds of our young men; a prestige that delayed our reawakening for long years, and still delays its completion or threatens to pervert its direction. The events of the past thirty-six years have confirmed in unmistakable language the truth of that statement. France still, as always, is self-deluded, believes herself to be the leader of European progress, and has from that time forth, almost of necessity, been moving in a circle, from monarchy to republicanism, from republicanism to despotism, and now she seems to be beginning the same revolution once again. Equally incapable of repose or normal motion; never able, whether under monarchy or republic, at home or abroad, to take one of those upward steps that open out a new horizon to nations already organized, or point an easier way for peoples wandering in search of a life as yet denied them. Nevertheless, the idea of France, mistress of the destinies of Europe and hastening to unfold them for the good of all, ploughs today like lightning through the soul of the young Italian generation, even as, when I faced the first battles and sorrows of life, it dominated the soul of the generation that is now dead or in lethargic old age. In each convulsive movement of France's great fall our people dream that initiative is reborn. Any thought that takes shape for a few days in Paris, even when it proves the dissolution of the old power which was based upon unity and the prevailing anarchy, finds among us thoughtless and indiscriminating applause. And at every fresh disillusioning, Italian lips utter, or Italian faces show, the cowardly thought: how should we attempt what France has failed to do. . . . Italy does not lack force, but the consciousness of the force that she has within herself; she lacks collective virtue; the trust of each city in its neighbour city, of each individual in his brother;

the trust of all in the latent life that throbs in the tradition of a people that once was great and is fated to be great again, the life that makes a nation.

Mazzini's view of the French endeavour would seem to have overlooked the enduring significance of the Declaration of the Rights of Man. But his concern was with the Duties of Man (the title he gave to his best known essay) – as it needed to be, until the country could be unified and a single constitution made effective throughout the land. From 1797 to 1849 there had been not one but twenty-three constitutions or fundamental statutes in force in the different kingdoms and dukedoms of Italy. There was little liberalism about any of them, until King Charles Albert of the House of Piedmont-Savoy promulgated on 4 March 1848 the promised 'statuto-fondamentale' of Sardinia (a kingdom which had been acquired by Piedmont from Spain in 1720). It was this fundamental law of the kingdom of Sardinia that became the constitutional law of the whole of Italy, and remained so until after the Second World War, in 1947.

What happened was that the impetus for the unification of Italy in the 1850s, which established the Kings of Sardinia (of the House of Piedmont-Savoy) as the Kings of Italy (by a law of 17 March 1861) and transferred the capital of the kingdom to Rome (by a law of 3 February 1871), led also to the imposition by decree of the fundamental law of Sardinia on each territory that came successively to be included in the Kingdom of Italy. On the overthrow in 1859 of the Austrians, with the help of the Emperor of France, Lombardy was joined to Piedmont; the peoples of Parma, Modena and Tuscany, given their own free choice, speedily voted their annexation to Piedmont; the people of the Papal States did the same, except in Rome and its immediate territory; meantime a revolution in Sicily against the Neapolitan Bourbons was brought to finality by the omnipresent Garibaldi who overthrew the Bourbon Government in Sicily and Naples alike; King Victor Emmanuel, advancing with the Italian troops on Naples, joined up with the popular leader, Garibaldi, near that city. The political unification of Italy was then complete, except for Venetia and the small territory of Rome itself. In 1866, after the new Italy had joined Prussia in a war on Austria,

Venetia also was added to the Kingdom of Italy – and the fundamental law of Sardinia became that of the whole country. Meantime, the first of the two legal codes regulating the ordinary life of the Italian people, as distinct from the constitution under which they were to be governed, had come into force on 1 January 1866. They were the Civil Code and the Commercial Code.

Italy was thus never a federated state like the German Reich of 1871. To that extent the reception of treaty law into the internal system is simpler. But Italy, like Germany, passed through a period of dictatorship, when the fundamental law was violently overridden, and its liberalism replaced by the compulsions requisite in a corporative State. A law of 24 December 1925, for example, made it necessary to obtain the consent of the head of the Government for the placing of any matter on the agenda of either of the legislative chambers; on 21 April 1927, a Charter of Labour defined the organization of the corporative State; on 21 March 1930, a new law made provision for the organization of a national council of corporations; even the revised Civil Code (with which is now combined the Commercial Code) enacted under the fascist dictatorship in 1942, bears traces of the régime's activities – though the continuity of the ordinary law contained in this code with that of its predecessors has emerged remarkably unscathed in the same way as did the ordinary law of Germany from the constitutional upheaval through which that country passed.

In June 1944, the King made over the royal powers to the Crown Prince, who became Lieutenant General of the Realm. But several political parties opposed Monarchy and, following an election held in 1946, a Republic was declared. The Lieutenant General left the country. Meantime the country had long since turned its back on the dictator. Mussolini, for some time in hiding, was done to death on 28 April 1945. A constituent assembly approved a new constitution on 22 December 1947. It was promulgated on 27 December and became effective on 1 January 1948.

As a legal portrait of a relatively young nation, and to be in character, the constitution needed to reflect, and does reflect, something of the historical antecedents of its present unity and something of the forward-looking aspirations of youth. The historical antecedents, one may feel, are well reflected in the division of the 'democratic republic based on labour' (Article 1) into 'regions . . . established as autonomous bodies having their own powers and functions . . . Special forms and conditions of autonomy are granted to Sicily, Sardinia, Trent-Upper Adige, Friulia, Venezia-Giulia and the Val d'Aosta' (Articles 115 and 116). Here is recognition of the diverse historical experience and racial make-up of the various parts of Italy that came together in the middle of the nineteenth century. Nevertheless, it is 'the Republic, one and indivisible' that 'recognizes and promotes local autonomies' (Article 5). The fact of its doing so does not – as has just been mentioned – create the same sort of problem for the reception of treaty law into internal law as arises in the case of a federated state such as Western Germany. Having laid down as part of the very first 'fundamental principle' that 'sovereignty belongs to the people', it is as if with a backward glance over its shoulder at Mazzini that the constitution entitles its all-important and forward-looking Part 1 the 'Rights and Duties of Citizens'.

At this point it is convenient to note what these are. The constitution provides for equality of all citizens before the law; protection of linguistic minorities; freedom of religion; inviolability of personal liberty and of personal domicile; freedom and secrecy of correspondence and other forms of communication; freedom of movement of citizens within the national territory as well as the right to leave and re-enter it; the right of peaceful assembly; the right of association; freedom of speech and of the press; the right of petition for the passing of legislation; immunity from deprivation of judicial status or citizenship for political reasons, from personal service or property levy except by virtue of law, from punishment under retroactive laws, and from the death penalty except under the laws of war. 'The Republic protects health as a fundamental right of the individual'; makes art and science and the teaching thereof free; provides primary education, compulsory and free of charge for at least eight years; and 'protects labour in all its forms and applications'. The right to maintenance and social assistance is assured to every citizen who is 'unable to work and without means of support necessary to life'. Private economic initiative is unrestricted, and 'private property is recognized and guaranteed by law'. 'All citizens of both sexes having attained the age of majority have the right to vote.'

With a constitutional basis such as this, Italy could, and did, ratify the Statute of the Council of Europe on 3 August 1949; the 'Protocol modifying and completing the Brussels Treaty' (i.e. of Western European Union) on 20 April 1955; the Convention of European Economic Cooperation on 24 August 1948; the European Convention of Human Rights on 26 October 1955; and it signed, together with all the other negotiating governments, the O.E.C.D. convention on 14 December 1960.

None of these international agreements makes a direct impact on the ordinary internal law or on the Constitution of Italy, any more than they do on those of other countries that ratify them. The European Community treaties, on the other hand, do of course make an impact on the ordinary internal law in Italy, as in the other countries of the Six. They have also, in Italy, caused difficult constitutional questions to arise. It is desirable to appreciate why this should be so.

The Italian Constitution of 1948 is a closely knit instrument of safeguard and control. The political history of Italy, the tribulations through which the country had passed, the twenty-year period of dictatorial rule made possible only by neglect of the originally Sardinian fundamental law which had become the constitution of unified Italy – all these factors help to explain not merely the closely knit system of checks and balances embodied in the 1948 constitution, but also the circumspect regard for its protection with which Italian judges (like their German opposite numbers) approach any legal problem that has a bearing on it. As a legal portrait of the nation, the Constitution itself not only reflects the historical antecedents of unification and the forward-looking aspirations of youth, but also a tense determination to preserve on an enduring basis the present character of the nation.

A special chapter of the constitution is devoted to 'Constitutional Guarantees'. It establishes a Constitutional Court to judge, *inter alia*, 'disputes concerning the constitutional legality of laws, and of acts having force of law enacted by the State and the regions'; as well as conflicts of jurisdiction between the (three) powers of the State ...' (Article 134). 'The Republican form of Government cannot be the subject of constitutional revision' (Article 139) but laws for the revision of the constitution in other ways may be adopted by absolute majority vote of each of the two chambers (Chamber of Deputies and Senate). However, unless on the second sitting of each chamber the revising law is approved by at least two thirds of the members, it may within three months of publication be submitted to popular referendum. A demand for a referendum in these circumstances may be made by any 500,000 voters, or by any five regional councils, or by one fifth of the members of either chamber (Article 138). These provisions, taken together, represent one of the most far-reaching attempts in the world today to afford the people themselves a direct rather an indirect role in the process of protection of a national constitution.

The ultimate alternative sanction of popular referendum, for a constitution-revising law, has something of a counterpart in the faculty granted the people themselves to introduce Bills for ordinary legislation into Parliament: 'The people may initiate laws by the submission, on the part of at least 50,000 voters, of draft laws drawn up in articles' (Article 71). The actual legislative function is of course exercised collectively by the two chambers, in which either the Government, or any single member of either chamber, or any body or agency on which the right to do so is conferred by constitutional law, may introduce a Bill (Articles 70 and 71).

When an international treaty entails, for example, a modification in the ordinary law of Italy (that is, other than the constitutional law) the authorization for the modification rests with the chambers. Their authorization takes the form of a law approving and implementing the treaty in question (Article 80). The treaty as such is ratified (for international purposes) by the President of the Republic (Article 87). (The President is elected for a term of seven years and 'before assuming his functions ... takes an oath of fidelity to the Republic and of observance of the Constitution, before Parliament sitting in joint session' – Article 91.)

At first sight it might appear that ratification, approval and implementation of the community treaties by Italy would not meet with any particular obstacles. Article 10 (1) of the Constitution states that 'the Italian legal system conforms to generally recognized principles of international law'. Article 11 provides that 'Italy agrees, on conditions of equality with other States, to the limitations of her sovereignty necessary to an organization which will assure peace and justice among nations, and promote and encourage international organizations constituted for this purpose'. The Parliament passed a law on 10 October 1957 approving the ratification of the E.E.C. and Euratom Treaties; Italy had similarly become a member of the Coal and Steel Community in 1951.

A few years after 1957 the electricity industry of Italy was nationalized by a law creating the public corporation called ENEL (Ente Nazionale Energia Elettrica). Very soon afterwards an Italian court found itself faced with the question whether this nationalization law was consistent with the E.E.C. Treaty. The question was referred to the Italian Constitutional Court. This court recognized that the conclusion of treaties limiting sovereignty was lawful and that the internal implementation of such a treaty could be on the basis of an ordinary law. It added that, in its opinion, Article 11 of the Constitution did not confer any special or privileged status upon the law approving the treaty.

From this it would of course follow that a subsequent internal and ordinary law could with impunity run counter to a preceding ordinary law made in implementation of a treaty. So the electricity nationalization law could legally defeat the internal application of the E.E.C. Treaty. Against this view, the Court of Justice of the European Communities expressed itself strongly when the question was before it. In its judgment of 15 July 1964 it ruled:

As opposed to other international treaties, the treaty instituting the E.E.C. has created its own order, which was integrated with the national order of the member States when the treaty came into force; as such, it is binding upon them.

In fact, by creating a Community of unlimited duration, having its own institutions, its own personality and its own capacity in law, apart from having international standing and, more particularly, real powers resulting from a limitation of competence or a transfer of powers from the States to the Community, the member States, albeit within limited spheres, have restricted their sovereign rights and created a body of law applicable both to their nationals and to themselves.

The reception, within the laws of each member State, of provisions having a Community source, and more particularly of the terms and of the spirit of the treaty, has as a corollary the impossibility, for the member State, to give preference to a unilateral and subsequent measure against a legal order accepted by them on a basis of reciprocity.

This particular lawsuit was settled when, in May 1966, the Milanese court, which had referred to the Communities' Court for a preliminary ruling, duly implemented the ruling just quoted. But the Milanese decision does not constitute a strict precedent (in the sense familiar to a British lawyer) that any other Italian court is *bound* to follow. Since, moreover, the decision has encountered much doctrinal criticism in Italy, it may not be possible to regard the general question to which it relates as being finally closed.

Meantime, in June 1964, the courts of Naples, Rome, Milan and Mondovi had been confronted with the argument that the procedure followed in Italy for approving and implementing the Coal and Steel Community treaty should have been that for passing constitutional laws (i.e. Article 138 – see above) and not that for passing ordinary laws. This was the argument advanced by several Italian industrial undertakings in asking these Italian courts to delay giving effect to a decision of the High Authority of the Coal and Steel Community, of which the undertakings were the subject. The Italian courts ruled that provision was made (or implied) in Article 11 of the Constitution for Parliament to pass an ordinary law for the approval and ratification of a treaty limiting the sovereignty of the Italian Republic. So they arrived at the same result as the Italian Constitutional Court.

The court of Turin was faced with a similar problem, on which it gave judgment on 11 December 1964. An Italian steel company appealed against a fine imposed by the High Authority because it had refused to comply with a request to forward the invoices relating to its electricity consumption during the period 1 April 1954 to 10 November 1958. It asked for the matter to be referred to the Italian Constitutional Court, submitting that the E.C.S.C. treaty had become incorporated in the Italian legal system as a result of an ordinary law, and not in compliance with the special procedure laid down in Article 138 of the Constitution, as it should have been. The case was referred to the Constitutional Court. The Turin court had considered that the submission as to unconstitutionality was clearly not without some foundation. For one thing, as a result and in respect of the E.C.S.C. treaty the judicial function in Italy was no longer exercised by the ordinary judges, as Article 102 of the Constitution required, but by the Court of Justice of the European Communities. For another thing, Article 113 of the Constitution provided for 'judicial protection ... against acts of the public administration ... before the organs of the ordinary and administrative jurisdiction' of Italy. A year later, in December 1965, the Italian Constitutional Court declared unfounded the suggestion of constitutional illegality relating to Articles 102 and 113 of the constitution – largely for the reason that the Italian internal legal order was distinct from the legal order of the Communities.

All such constitutional matters will need to be (and are in course of being) determined finally by the Italian authorities, if community law is to enjoy the paramountcy over internal law that was the intention of the treaty makers, and if the process of community integration is to proceed smoothly.

Apart from these constitutional aspects it is necessary to consider the means at the disposal of the Italian Government for the implementing (i) of those provisions of the community treaties which have direct internal application, (ii) of the community regulations made by virtue of the treaties, and (iii) of community directives. The Constitution does not in general favour the Government exercising the legislative function, or issuing decrees having the force of ordinary laws. But exceptions are provided in both cases.

Article 76 provides:

The exercise of the legislative function cannot be delegated to the Government unless guiding principles and standards have been specified and only for a limited time and for definite objectives.

Article 77 provides:

The Government may not issue decrees having the force of ordinary laws without the authorization of the Chambers. When, in extraordinary cases of necessity and urgency, the Government, on its own responsibility adopts provisional measures having the force of law, it must on the same day present them to the Chambers for conversion into law. Should the Chambers be in recess, they shall be expressly convoked and meet within five days. Decrees lose their efficacy as of their date of issue if not converted into law within sixty days of their publication.

In these two articles are to be found yet further examples of the safeguards against arbitrary government which, understandably, permeate the whole of the Italian Constitution of 1948. At the same time they include the exceptions which enable the Government to meet the exigencies of the community treaties.

According to the type or subject-matter of community law with which they are concerned, the Italian authorities must, in practice, decide whether to implement it internally either by a law, or by a regulation, or by a simple administrative act. When Parliament passed the law of 14 October 1957 approving the ratification of the E.E.C. and Euratom Treaties, in accordance with Article 76 of the Constitution, it authorized the Government to issue, without parliamentary supervision, decrees having the force of law, in order to implement certain obligations under the treaties or to give effect to certain measures provided for in them.

This parliamentary authorization expired on 31 December 1961. During the period from 1 January 1962 to 13 July 1965 there was no delegation of legislative power, in the full sense, by Parliament to the Government. When it had to take implementing measures in application of Article 10 of the E.E.C. Treaty the Government did not revert to the procedure of itself initiating parliamentary legislation, as it might have done. It preferred the method of 'provisional' measures, in the form of administrative circulars issued by the Minister of Finance, pending a law giving them retroactive effect.

On 13 July 1965 (by law no. 871) Parliament again delegated legislative powers to the Government with respect to matters covered by the E.E.C. and Euratom Treaties. The delegation was made effective for the duration of the second stage of the Common Market's transitional period.

Italian *regulations* were made to give effect to the Common Market's common external tariff. Power was delegated by Parliament to the Government for this purpose by law no. 1527 of 20 December 1960, but regulations issued by virtue of this law had to have the prior opinion of a parliamentary committee (set up in 1949) composed of senators and deputies, with responsibility for advising the Government on measures taken in the customs tariff sector under a delegation of powers.

The law of 1960 did not, however, apply to measures by which the Government might carry out its obligations with regard to customs duties under Article 11 of the E.E.C. Treaty. So the Government had to resort to the procedure for securing parliamentary *legislation* for this purpose. Law no. 13 of 1965 delegated powers to the Government to introduce the new customs tariffs.

In order to adopt the E.E.C. common agricultural policy the Italian Government used the emergency procedure available to it under Article 77 of the Constitution (see above). It did so, too, in decree-law no. 939 of 23 October 1964, in order to give effect to the E.E.C. Council decision of 8 May 1964, concerning the common external tariff for petroleum and mineral oils.

A simple presidential decree (22 September 1963) based on Article 5 of the E.E.C. Treaty was used to give effect to Article 13 of E.E.C. Regulation no. 17. (This is the article which authorizes the competent authorities of the member States, at the request of the European Commission, to carry out investigations into the affairs of undertakings and associations of undertakings in order to see if they are conforming to the free competition and anti-monopoly rules of the E.E.C. Treaty.)

From all the foregoing, the impression will be gained that in

Italy, as in Western Germany, doubts about the paramountcy of community law over internal law, and even perhaps the somewhat restrictive way in which the Government has been authorized to implement the treaty provisions, regulations and decisions, have resulted in a certain lack of readiness – in the legal sphere – to integrate freely into the Communities. By comparison with the other extreme of Holland and Luxemburg, even with France, this is perhaps true. Such comparisons, are, however, no less odious than others and are in any event particularly difficult to make with any degree of real accuracy in this particular context. So far as the hesitancy in Western Germany and Italy represents jealous regard for the constitution, it is surely explicable – and also desirable, provided the hesitancy can be satisfactorily overcome. It is a good thing that in Italy as in Western Germany the whole of the Judiciary, by dint of its complete independence of the other two powers in the State – the Executive and the Legislature – can contribute its share to the upholding of the constitution, of which the Constitutional Court provides the guarantee of last resort. It is also a good thing that the Legislature should exercise sparingly its right to confer legislative power, or its equivalent, upon the Executive. Given the complexity of modern government such conferment is doubtless inevitable; but how best to preserve safeguards against abuse of the power so conferred is a problem facing all the western democracies in some degree, Britain included.

In the sphere of administrative law, Italy in the 1950s was not far behind the French advance. Its system was well developed and a tribunal of the same name as the French Council of State had been confirmed by the 1948 constitution as the supreme arbiter in these matters. 'Jurisdiction to protect legitimate interests with regard to the public administration shall be vested in the Council of State and other organs of administrative justice. In certain cases determined by law, such jurisdiction shall extend to subjective rights' states Article 103. Quick to recognize the protection against legally unwarranted actions of the High Authority that was provided by the administrative law remedies embodied in the Coal and Steel Community Treaty, the Italian Government and associations of Italian industrial undertakings were together responsible for four out of a total of six lawsuits brought on this basis against the High Authority in the very first year of activity of the Community's Court of Justice, 1954–5.

LUXEMBURG

This little country, of 1,000 square miles and some 350,000 citizens, most of whose territory today forms part of the table-land of the Ardennes, had lost its political independence as early as 1443. Some 350 years later, at the end of the eighteenth century, it found itself annexed to Napoleon's France with the suitable descriptive name of 'Department of the Forests'. Came the Treaty of Vienna in 1815. Luxemburg, part-amputated by the loss of all territory beyond the rivers Sûre and Our, was ceded to the King of the Netherlands and his successors, to possess in perpetuity the full property and sovereignty over it. The King added to his royal titles that of Grand Duke of Luxemburg, and the Grand Duchy became, as intended, one of the member States of the Germanic Confederation. Its independence (subject only to membership of the Confederation, which Vienna contemplated) was not, however, realized. For, by action of the King, the fundamental law of the Kingdom of the Netherlands – saving special provisions for the relations of the Grand Duchy with the Germanic Confederation – was made to apply to it. However, at least a beginning had been made in restoring political indepen-dence for the Grand Duchy. It was not until 31 December 1830 that William the First decreed that Luxemburg would be governed 'distinctly and separately from the Kingdom of the Netherlands'. But at that time the new régime could in fact be made applicable only in the capital, because the rest of the country had made common cause with the provisional government of Brussels, which, on 3 October, had proclaimed Belgium's independence of the Netherlands.

There followed the Treaty of London in April 1839, by which the Grand Duchy lost two-thirds of its territory but finally regained its independence. It remained however, a member State of the Germanic Confederation. In 1841 the Grand Duke granted the country a constitution 'in harmony with the statutes of the Confederation', which meant that sovereignty continued to reside in the person of the King–Grand Duke. The constitution was fragmentary and unsatisfactory – but it was nevertheless a constitution. There were to be 'States General' to conduct the country's affairs. But the election of deputies to the 'States' was indirect; its sittings were not held in public; and its powers were limited. It could do little more than issue opinions, though its assent was needed for laws to regulate crime, taxes and customs tariffs. It had the right to make administrative regulations, but these had to have the prior approval of the King–Grand Duke.

In 1848 the wave of revolts for independence, and of revolutions, that had been disturbing Europe since 1820, produced a corresponding ripple in Luxemburg. From March onwards there were revolts in the capital and in particular at Ettelbruck and Mersch. The Government took safety measures, and prepared to revise the constitution. The year (1848) that in February saw the Second Republic proclaimed in France, saw also little Luxemburg with a new constitution sanctioned by the King–Grand Duke on 9 July.

The new constitution reproduced in large part the Belgian Constitution of 1831, which has been described in a preceding part of this chapter. It was the first liberal constitution of Luxemburg but it was only to remain in force until 1856. The underlying reason for this was that it was out of tune with the statutes of the Germanic Confederation, and a strong reaction against it had been apparent in the German Diet.

The Speech from the Throne on 7 October 1856 was an appeal to the deputies to give favourable treatment to a project for constitutional revision 'in the spirit of moderation and wisdom of which you have always given proof, and with full regard to the monarchical sentiment, which is the hereditary political dogma of the Luxembourgeois'. The appeal was not heeded. After a long and passionate debate, an address in reply was voted. It reaffirmed the monarchical sentiments of the people of Luxemburg, but it expressed the hope 'that the former political liberties established in 1815, 1841 and 1848 by the illustrious House of Orange–Nassau, will not be taken from us to make way for a régime alien to our way of life and out of keeping with our degree of civilization'. The royal reaction was equally strong. As a result, on 28 October a motion of no confidence in the Government was passed. But the Cabinet would not resign. The majority of the deputies thereupon refused to attend the sittings. There followed a Royal–Grand Ducal decree on 27 November, ordering the dissolution of the Chamber and the entry into force of the new Constitution.

The explanatory preamble (to the project for revision) had been severely critical of the 1848 Constitution. It was 'a democratic Constitution which might suit a Republic'. It characterized the powers of the King–Grand Duke as constitutional 'rights', whereas these powers had their source in European treaties and in the mutual pacts, made Sovereign to Sovereign, which these treaties confirmed. Even with royal–grand ducal consent, the preamble argued, the Luxemburg Constitution could not modify the exercise of these sovereign rights to a greater extent than that permitted by the European treaties. Moreover, the 1848 Constitution set up three distinct powers. The fiction of three powers was only the application of the theory of the sovereignty of the people. But this theory could not be reconciled with the basic principle of the power of the monarchy, laid down particularly in Article 57 of the Final Act of Vienna in 1815. On this matter, the explanation affirmed

It is therefore necessary not merely that the internal constitution . . . should not substitute the personification of powers for the sovereignty of the Head of State, but also that whatever bodies and individuals may be called upon to participate in, or to cooperate with, the action of the Sovereign, they should never be seen as acting on the basis of any principle of their own [separate] existence, or as entirely independent of the Chief of State, and even less as a predominant power. They should only be seen as invested with a power to cooperate.

The reversal of the previous liberal trend seemed complete. The Grand Duke might well proclaim, on the same 27 November 1856:

Armed with Our Sovereign rights, fully conscious of Our duties towards Our Allies and towards Our subjects, We now and henceforward reassume the authority which is inseparable from Our Crown.

There was, however, one very important step forward. Anxious not just to substitute ministerial omnipotence for that of the former Chambers, but only to ensure that the Chamber should not continue to usurp the function of general administrator of the country, the 1856 Constitution introduced a balancing factor which had previously been lacking. It did so by establishing a Council of State, bearing considerable similarity to the French body of the same name *as it operated in the early part of the nineteenth century*.

The role of the Luxemburg Council of State, as defined in the 1856 Constitution, was threefold. In the first place it was legislative: to debate and discuss draft laws and any amendments made in them. Secondly, it was judicial: to determine conflicts of view as to which might be the competent body to carry out such and such an activity, to consider disputes concerning the legality of decrees and general regulations, and to determine lawsuits against the administration on the basis of administrative law. Thirdly, it was consultative: in respect of all matters which might be referred to it by the King–Grand Duke, or by the provisions of any law.

The intention of the 1856 constitution-maker, in introducing the Council of State, was not, primarily anyway, to afford legal protection for the interests of private citizens against those of the State, but rather to strengthen the hand of the Government, by setting up a barrier against the tendencies of the Chamber of Deputies (now once more an 'Assembly of the States') always to extend its activities into the sphere of administration. This was of course apparent to the Assembly. For a large section of its members, the Council of State, like the new constitution, remained for a considerable time an object of suspicious resistance. Very gradually, this was overcome; its role accepted, its powers extended. Under the impulse of more liberal ideas, and on the basis of experience gained, it was reorganized by a law of 16 January 1866. A major part of the reorganization was for the purpose of ensuring a more decisive role for the Council of State as the judge of the legality of administrative action, hence, as the protector of private interests against those of the State. Intrinsically the Luxemburg body was following, roughly speaking, the pattern of development pursued by its French counterpart. In this development lies the explanation why Luxemburg was able to accept readily the administrative law provisions contained in the three treaties establishing the European Communities in the 1950s. The Council of State was further modernized and strengthened by a law of 8 February 1961.

The 1856 Constitution had emphasized the principle that *executive* power reposed solely in the Grand Duke, while solemnly proclaiming, as has been shown, that all sovereign power was his alone. All reference to distinct powers in the Constitution was suppressed, apart from the express mention of executive power. Nevertheless, the constitution did provide that the assent of the Assembly of States was necessary for any law, and that justice was administered, in the name of the King–Grand Duke, by courts and tribunals composed of judges who were irremovable. By implication, the existence of the three distinct powers, of Executive, Legislature and Judiciary, was thereby admitted – and this was a principle that the Council of State has never called in question. The formula adopted in 1856 was preserved, moreover, when revisions of the constitution were effected in 1868 (following the dissolution of the Germanic Confederation in 1866) and in 1919.

Furthermore, the provision attributing all sovereign power to the King–Grand Duke was removed in 1868, and replaced, in 1919, by a declaration of the sovereignty of the nation. It may well be that the constitution-makers of 1919 intended this as a declaration of the sovereignty of the people, represented by the Chamber of Deputies, because the words 'nation' and 'people' are both used frequently as if interchangeable. Certainly the *concept* of 'nation' was changed in 1919, when universal suffrage was made constitutional, the right to vote being granted to all persons of both sexes who had attained the age of twenty-one.

The Constitution of 1868 had restored most of the principles contained in the 1848 Constitution, of Belgian inspiration. It is still in force today, though amended in some important respects (in 1919, with the affirmation of popular democracy; in 1948, with the abolition of neutrality and the guarantee of economic and social rights; in 1956, in respect of international relations). However, some leading Luxemburg authorities* take the view that, on a correct reading of the texts, none of the attributes of sovereignty yet pertains wholly to the people through their representatives. As in the past, the Grand Duke alone possesses executive power; the legislative power, as in the past, is shared between the Grand Duke and the Chamber; justice is administered by the courts and tribunals in the name of the Grand Duke. Nevertheless, some role is reserved for direct government by the people by way of referendum.

So, from all the foregoing, there emerges a constitutional portrait of Luxemburg showing strong traits of character, for which historical antecedents and interplay of influences are responsible: government by France, by the Netherlands, the necessity at one period to remain aligned to the Germanic Confederation, the strong pull of Belgium. Besides this constitutional aspect, in respect of matters of private law, Luxemburg had been, from very early times, within the sphere of influence of France. Indeed the Napoleonic Civil Code, which was introduced into Luxemburg by law in 1804, still forms the basis of Luxemburg private law today. Again, it was on the French model that the Council of State was established in 1856; and the case law it has developed in disputes between private interests and those of the State has found external inspiration, when necessary, not only in the jurisprudence of its French opposite number, but also in the administrative law built up by the ordinary courts of Belgium. We can also note that the law which today governs the conservation of the forests of Luxemburg is a seventeenth-century law given her by Austria, which works so satisfactorily there is no point in changing it. Then we can understand the particular strength of the legal soul of this little country more clearly. Drawing on a considerable variety of sources, Luxemburg seems to have selected the best and, adding her particular contribution, made the results markedly her own.

*See, for example, Felix Welter in *Le Livre Jubilaire du Conseil d'État du Grand Duché de Luxembourg*, 1957, p. 72.

In 1948, by way of legal protection of private interests in the face of the continually increasing intervention of the State in all aspects of the country's affairs, the 'Rights of Luxemburgers', expressly inscribed in the constitution, were considerably extended (particularly in Articles 11 and 23). The Constitution now provides for equality before the law, individual liberty, the right to property, inviolability of domicile, abolition of the death penalty in political matters, freedom of religion, free and compulsory primary education, freedom of speech and of the press, the right to peaceful assembly, the right to form associations, the right to petition and secrecy of correspondence.

So there emerged, from German occupation and the destruction of war, as a representative democracy with a constitutional monarch, the 'free, independent and indivisible' State which is Luxemburg today.

Getting quickly to its feet, it renounced the meaningless neutrality which had been imposed upon it by the Treaty of London, 1867. It became a founding member of the Council of Europe, the Statute of which it ratified on 3 August 1949; with Belgium, France, the Netherlands and Britain, it set up the Brussels Treaty Organization in 1948, and continued as a member when it was enlarged into Western European Union in 1954; it participated from the outset in establishing the Convention of European Economic Cooperation, which it ratified on 14 April 1949, and continued as a member when this was modified and enlarged to become the O.E.C.D. Convention in 1960; meantime, in 1953, it had ratified the European Convention on Human Rights. It did not, therefore, lag behind in the process of European unification through co-operation, but was well in step with the rest of Western Europe. None of these treaties and conventions posed problems for the constitutional law of the country, or had any *direct* impact on the body of ordinary law by which the lives of Luxemburgers are regulated – any more than for the citizens of the other European (or Scandinavian) States that adhered to them. As in other countries the treaties produced economic benefits, inaugurated a novel principle for the protection of human rights, and imposed an obligation on the citizen, on the occurrence of certain specified contingencies, to join in a collective system of self-defence. In all this, the Luxemburgers could hardly feel there was any threat to the fulfilment of the instinctive wish that is expressed in their national saying: 'We want to stay as we are' ('Mir woelle bleiwe wat mir sin').

Such a frame of mind is assuredly not strictly relevant, as a matter of law, to the question that follows; but it does seem to import a particular flavour to it. What is the effect of treaties of *integration* entered into by Luxemburg, upon the body of ordinary and constitutional law under which her people live? At the present time this question concerns the European Community Treaties, to all three of which Luxemburg was an original adherent. But, in a sense, the whole of her history as an independent State since the nineteenth century had prepared the country to absorb more readily than any of the other five members the strictly legal consequences of membership. By the force of circumstances, Luxemburg had never been able to conceive of her national sovereignty in such stark and absolute terms as had been elsewhere induced on the emergence of the modern nation States of Western Europe. While striving to establish her international personality, to become and 'to remain what we are', Luxemburg was necessarily practising the legal arts of combining the effects of national sovereignty – from the moment she ultimately attained it – with the internal results of international treaties or arrangements to which she was inevitably a party. Early nineteenth-century experience, before her full independence, of membership of the Germanic Confederation, and then of the German Customs Union (Zollverein); in the mid nineteenth century, a railway network – constructed, thanks to French capital, by the Société Guillaume (Luxembourg) – operated, under concession, by the French Compagnie de l'Est; in 1871, after the Franco–Prussian war, a cession of the operating rights to the German Reich, which, by treaty with Luxemburg in 1872, linked the railway network to that of Alsace–Lorraine, while undertaking to respect Luxemburg neutrality and at the same time recognizing not only the right of supervision by Luxemburg of the network on her territory, but also the jurisdiction of her courts over disputes arising from it; then, following its establishment in 1921, operation of the Belgo–Luxemburg Economic Union – all these experiences, and others, early introduced Luxemburg to the internal legal effect of treaties of integration, and prepared her well for the operation of the European Coal and Steel Community Treaty from the beginning of 1952.

It was, in fact, with the two Rome Treaties of E.E.C. and Euratom in mind that in October 1956 Luxemburg made more explicit and complete the provisions regulating treaty-making that the constitution contains. 'The Grand Duke makes treaties. Treaties shall not take effect until approved by law and published in the manner prescribed for the publication of laws.' Every law has to have the approval of the Chamber of Deputies. A treaty law, like any ordinary law, is put to the Chamber by the Grand Duke. But where a treaty is concerned with what the Constitution calls 'International Powers' the law for its approval cannot be debated and passed, except by the special procedures required for revising the constitution itself. That is to say, the draft law cannot be debated unless at least three quarters of the members of the Chamber are present, or passed unless a vote of at least two thirds of those present approves of it (Article 115). So for a treaty of this particular kind (such as the European Community Treaties) the maximum safeguard in the constitution ensures the defence of the internal law of Luxemburg. 'International Powers' is a descriptive section-heading introduced for the first time into the constitution in 1956. There is only one article (49^2) under this heading, and it, too, is completely new. The careful wording of it must surely indicate that its clear-headed drafters could not be beguiled by ill-digested notions of 'surrender of sovereignty'. It reads:

The exercise of functions reserved by the Constitution to the legislative, executive and judicial powers may be temporarily delegated by treaty to institutions of international law.

The institutions of the European Communities (the Council, Commission, Court of Justice, and Parliament) are such institutions.

When a treaty has been approved by a law passed by the Chamber of Deputies, the implementation of the treaty within Luxemburg is effected not by Parliament but by the Executive.

The Grand Duke issues the regulations and orders necessary to give effect to treaties and does so in the manner requisite for measures giving effect to laws, to which measures they have equivalent effect, without prejudice to those matters for which the Constitution requires a law. (Concluding paragraph of Article 37, newly added in 1956.)

Sometimes, as the last phrase of this quotation shows, a covering law, other than the law approving the treaty, may be necessary for the Executive to act in this way. But there is no need for legislation by 'Parliament' dealing *directly* with the *details* of treaty implementation. In this respect, Luxemburg handles treaty implementation in a more clear-cut fashion than some other Western European countries.

This explains why, for the purpose of giving effect to the Regulations, Decisions, Directives, Opinions and Recommendations in the sphere of agriculture, made by the European Economic Community, this was done by the Grand Ducal Regulation of 28 July 1962 (later replaced by the Grand Ducal Regulation of 17 August 1965).* These implementing measures concerning agriculture were issued under an emergency procedure under which the Luxemburg Government did not even need to consult the Council of State. On the other hand, when it was a matter of implementing in Luxemburg the controls on competition (set up by certain Articles of Regulation No. 17 of the European Economic Community), there *was* prior consultation between the Luxemburg Council of State and the E.E.C. Commission before the Grand Ducal Regulation of 26 May 1965 was issued.

Luxemburg orders and regulations of minor importance, which implement *provisions of the Community treaties* having direct internal application, or Community *regulations*, will similarly be made by the Executive. But they may be thus made by virtue not only of the treaty provisions or community regulations concerned but also of a Luxemburg law enabling the Executive so to act. An example of such an enabling law is that of 6 June 1923 (superseded by the law of August 1963, and amplified by that of 19 June 1965) dealing with the import, export and re-export of goods. It confers very wide powers on the Executive in the sphere of external trade.

* See Memorial 1962, A.P. 646, and Memorial 1963, A.P. 766.

Directives of E.E.C. and Euratom, and *recommendations* of E.C.S.C., are given effect to in Luxemburg in two ways, according to whether the subject-matter of the directive lies within the authority of the Luxemburg Executive or not. If the Executive has no authority in respect of the subject-matter of the directive, it can be given effect to in Luxemburg by means of legislation – but as yet there are no examples of this, no doubt because of the far reaching authorization already given to the Executive. There is, indeed, a law conferring 'full powers' (loi de pleins pouvoirs) renewed from year to year, and authorizing the Head of State to take any *economic* measure in the form of a regulation (arrêté réglementaire), after the Council of State has been consulted and the consent of a parliamentary committee obtained. This is a procedure of law-making (rule-making) to which the Executive frequently has recourse. Indeed the suggestion is now being made in Luxemburg that the Chamber of Deputies should give the Executive a general authorization to take any measures necessary to implement *all* community directives, irrespective of the subject-matter they deal with. Meantime, Luxemburg enabling laws, of particular or limited scope, make it readily possible to give internal effect to community directives. Examples are (1) the Luxemburg law of 30 June 1961, permitting the taking of any general measures relating to prices; (2) the Luxemburg law of 25 September 1963, concerning the control of foodstuffs; this enabled the Executive to give effect to the E.E.C. directive of 23 October by the use of a Grand Ducal regulation of 28 February 1964; (3) the Luxemburg law of 25 March 1963, which contained provisions for protection against the hazards of ionizing radiations, also enabled the Euratom directive of 2 February 1959 on this matter to be put into effect within Luxemburg.

Community *decisions* may be enforced in Luxemburg in one of two ways. Community decisions on tariffs are given effect to in Luxemburg by the methods that apply to the Belgo–Luxemburg Economic Union. Put simply, it is merely a matter of confirmation by the Grand Duchy of legislation and regulations introduced in Belgium. Community decisions addressed directly to individuals and corporate bodies, on the other hand, are covered by the Grand Ducal Regulation of 17 October 1962 providing for the implementation in Luxemburg of community decisions – including judgments of the Communities' Court of Justice. (This regulation replaces the Grand Ducal Order of 28 March 1955 relating to the decisions and judgments of E.C.S.C. The authenticity of Community decisions and judgments is checked and certified by the Luxemburg Minister of Foreign Affairs. Thereupon, an enforcement order is made by the Luxemburg Minister of Justice.)

From the foregoing, it would certainly seem that in Luxemburg there is no particular constitutional difficulty in the way of the internal implementation of community law. On the more fundamental question of general principle – the paramountcy of community law over ordinary internal law – there is no direct guidance in the Luxemburg Constitution. On the other hand, the consistent decisions of the Luxemburg courts, following a judgment of the Supreme Court of Justice in 1954, and the concurrence of legal doctrine with those decisions, makes it appear incontrovertible in Luxemburg law, that any international treaty confirmed by internal law is paramount over the ordinary internal law. This is a question which has caused some difficulties in other countries of the Six, as has been shown.

THE NETHERLANDS

For each of the nations which have so far occupied a section in this chapter it has been relatively easy to start from a date, or with a period, when its modern legal character began to take shape. At some risk of missing historical antecedents of importance, this is an approach which seemed to give a reasonably accurate portrait of the nations now engaged in a process of unification. Belgium could be looked at from the moment of her revolt and breakaway from Holland in 1830. France, from the period of the overthrow of despotism, and the beginning of the oscillations, since repeated, between some form or degree of caesarism and some form or degree of republicanism. Western Germany, from 1949, the date of the Basic Law; though, for the legal portrait of modern Germany to have depth and proportion it seemed essential to sketch in the earlier background, particularly since 1870; for Italy, it was the struggle for unification in the mid nineteenth century that began to fashion the modern legal character of that nation; Luxemburg, always at the focal point of divergent political influences throughout her history, seemed to need a more analytical legal portrait conceived in terms of that history.

For the Netherlands, there is some temptation to start with 1813, when William, the last Stadholder, was restored as 'sovereign prince' – or from 1815, when, at the Congress of Vienna, Holland and Belgium were formed into a single State under his sovereignty as King. Indeed, to this day, Holland (to use the popular name for the Netherlands) lives under the Constitution of 1815, as subsequently amended, so that to start with that date seems at first sight justifiable. Yet the breakaway of Belgium a mere fifteen years later reveals the artificiality of the 1815 political arrangement, and prompts the seeker after a true legal portrait of the Netherlands to probe deeper. It is then that in all the long, rich and varied legal history of the country, it becomes a baffling exercise to find a date – even a period – with which to begin.

Perhaps it is better so. Like Britain, the country found and developed its legal soul over a very long period of history. But whereas in Britain the work of rugged individualism in perfecting that continuous development could proceed undisturbed within the protection of the encircling seas, the Netherlands were so often dominated, for lengthy periods, by one external power or another that the similar human qualities which there exist could not be displayed in a similar way or to a similar effect. Yet there was outstanding achievement, in the legal sphere as in others, whether in times of active domination and oppression, or in times of relative freedom from it.

It was on the island of Betuwe, between the Rhine and the Waal, that there settled the earliest inhabitants of Holland known to recorded history. They were the Batavi. It is known that they furnished a contingent to the Roman armies who had reduced the Belgae. Then, in the fourth century came first the Salic Franks, then the Frisians, then the Saxons, overrunning the country. Merging with the Frisians, the Batavi also began to occupy the coastal regions. Four centuries later the country was incorporated in the dominions of Charlemagne. But under his successors, who were weak rulers, feudalism developed. The most powerful lords were the Count of Holland and the Bishop of Utrecht in the north, the Duke of Brabant and the Count of Flanders in the south. Great stimulus to trade was given by the Crusades. The chartered towns waxed in strength. Bruges became the main depôt for the spices and other goods of the East. Trade with the Hanseatic League, and the growth of the woollen and linen manufacturers, all contributed to the wealth of the Flemish cities. There was no real hindrance to industry in the Netherlands until another foreign dominator, the House of Burgundy, gaining a footing in the country in 1384, set about consolidating the petty fiefs, and finally acquired possession of all the seventeen provinces. A bare century later, a Dutch 'Magna Carta' was wrested from the ruling Burgundians. This was the 'Great Privilege', as it was named. But it was set aside by the next ruler, and when Spain replaced the Burgundians it was submerged in the Inquisition, introduced in 1550.

By way of resistance to Spain there was formed the League of Arras. But the Protestant north preferred to make a separate union, and on 29 January 1579 there was signed the Union of Utrecht. The possibility of installing a monarch had been ruled out. Even after 1579 there seems to have been no conscious desire of the leaders of the northern provinces either for republicanism as an alternative, or for the independence of the country that would have made a choice between the two more necessary. Throughout the 200 years of the 'Dutch Republic', as the system was called, there was never a satisfactory and lasting adjustment between the powers of the royal lieutenants (the 'Stadholders'), who continued to exercise their executive functions, and the powers of the estates, among which the States of Holland were predominant. In consequence, there were revolutions in 1618, 1650, 1672, 1747 and 1787.

Yet in five energetic years following the formation of the Union of Utrecht, William the Silent, the 'Father of his Country', laid the foundations for the recognition of the Republic as a sovereign State. He was assassinated in 1584; but by 1596 the Dutch, French and English were entering into the Triple Alliance – thereby implicitly recognizing the sovereignty of the Netherlands. William had never liked the Union because he hoped to unite all the seventeen provinces of South and North in the war against Spain (that was to last thirty years). This being impossible, and realizing that the northern provinces could not be defended without foreign assistance, William offered the sovereignty of the Netherlands to the Duke of Anjou, brother of the French King. The Treaty of Plessy-les-Tours, in September 1580, set the seal on Anjou's acceptance, but reserved ultimate control of all important governmental matters to the States. Anjou became Duke of Brabant and of Gelderland, Count of Flanders and Lord of Friesland; but Holland and Zeeland distrusted him, as a Catholic, so that William had reluctantly to become Count of these provinces himself. A few months later the northern provinces solemnly repudiated the sovereignty of Philip II of Spain. In 1583, a discredited Anjou, who had attempted to wrest from the States powers to which the treaty did not entitle him, went to France with the intention of returning. But there he died. A year later William met his death.

His eldest son was in the hands of the Spaniards. His second son, Maurice of Nassau, was appointed the President of the newly constituted Council of State, and Stadholder of Holland and Zeeland. But he was as yet only seventeen, and the government had to be conducted on his behalf. The France of Henry III was in too weak a condition to be of help, and the Spaniards, under the Duke of Parma, took town after town. In 1585, after a protracted resistance, Antwerp finally fell, and Elizabeth of England, refusing the proffered sovereignty, dispatched troops under the Earl of Leicester. The year England will never forget – 1588 – the year of the Spanish Armada, brought some indirect relief to the Netherlands. In 1590, Maurice captured the town of Breda, and the counter-offensive against the Spaniards was under way. After some nineteen years there followed a twelve-year truce, ending in 1621.

The seventeenth century, no less than the sixteenth, and perhaps even more, was for the Dutch an epoch of war on all hands. War with Spain, resumed in 1621; war with the English, in 1652–4 and again in 1665; then, in 1672, Louis XIV brought a massive French force against the eastern frontiers. William of Orange, called to power in June of that year, was made Captain General of the Union and Stadholder of Zeeland and Holland. Under his leadership, the Dutch, by opening the dykes, brought the advancing French to a halt within a day's march of Amsterdam. Before the end of the year 1673, there was no longer any direct danger to the existence of the Republic. In 1687 came another war with France, which ended, this time, in the almost complete isolation of Louis XIV. Ten years previously William had married Mary, the elder daughter of the Duke of York, heir presumptive to the English throne; in 1688, William was invited to England by the Earl of Danby and other leading men. He landed at Torbay on 5 November. Seven weeks later James II finally left the country. Not willing to act as Regent, William agreed that he and Mary should become King and Queen of England. The first great Statute of their English reign was the previously agreed Bill of Rights – 'An Act Declaring the Rights and Liberties of the subject, and Settling the Succession of the Crowne'.

Not only in Western Europe were the Dutch in conflict in this period. At the beginning of the century the long fight with Spain had spread far beyond its original field of action to include semi-official hostilities in Far Eastern waters. Commercial rivalry was at the root of these battles, in which not only Spaniards but also Portuguese became engaged. For, like the Dutch, they found the Far East trade most profitable. So it came about that early in 1603 one Jacob Heemskerck, acting for an Amsterdam firm of shipowners, took captive the carack *Catherine*. This occurred before the States General of the Union had authorized Dutch and Zeeland Companies, trading in the Orient, to seize vessels and cargoes as prize. There followed a Prize Court hearing as to the legality of the seizure.

What is of interest for the present discussion is not so much the fact that some eighteen months later the captured property was declared to be good prize, as the course of events that then ensued. For, on the one hand, there was revealed the deeply ingrained love of peace of the Dutch people, for all their resolute determination to be free of foreign dominance, and, on the other hand, the same events called forth the creative genius of one of the greatest international lawyers of all time – Hugo Grotius. It is perhaps not stretching the imagination too far to see these two developments as marking out, three centuries in advance, the exceptional suitability of the Netherlands to be the forum for the debating of legal issues of world-wide importance (such as occurred with the Hague Conferences at the turn of the last century) as well as for the International Court of Justice, or World Court as it is popularly called, which has had its seat there since the end of the First World War. In much the same tradition it is, fittingly, the Netherlands Government that has for years convened the inter-governmental conferences on particular aspects of private international law. It was also the influence of the Netherlands, and especially of the great University of Leyden, whither many Scottish lawyers and students found their way, that helped to foster, from the fifteenth century onwards, the development of Scots law as a system of civil law – upon the general basis of Roman law, first positively received into Scotland in the eleventh century. Indeed at the period of history which the present narrative has now reached, the great Scots authority, Stair, was in exile in Leyden (1682–8), and his 'Institutes' of Scots law was in large measure the result.

To resume the narrative. When, in 1604, the Prize Court awarded most of the proceeds of the property captured from the *Catherine* to the 'Great United Company of the East Indies' (with which Heemskerck's Amsterdam firm had meantime merged), and when the government conferred the monopoly of the East Indian trade upon the same company in recognition of its services to the country (which had benefited handsomely in tax), there were shareholders who withdrew from the company. Disapproving of war under any circumstances, they refused to accept their share of the profits awarded by the court. One of these dissenting shareholders – most of whom belonged to the Mennonite sect – even went so far as to draw up a plan for a new organization which would devote its efforts to strictly peaceable commercial enterprise under the patronage of Henry IV of France.

This plan never came to fruition, but the mere threat of rivalry alarmed both the States General and the United Company, already embarrassed by widespread criticism in regard to prize. There was an urgent if momentary need for a defence of these policies. Between the autumn of 1604 and the spring of 1605 the precocious twenty-one-year-old Grotius wrote precisely such a defence, in his *Commentary on the Law of Prize and Booty* (*De Jure Praedae*). He had acted as advocate for the company in the Prize Court proceedings concerning the *Catherine*, and had an intimate knowledge of all the documents. Probably he wrote his commentary at the request of the company, but this is not known for certain. Anyway he did not publish it in full. But when a few years later, in the autumn of 1608, negotiations were under way for the truce with Spain which has been mentioned above, and became blocked by Spain's refusal to recognize the right of the Netherlands to engage in trade and navigation in the Orient, at that point Grotius stepped right into the intellectual fray. Revising one chapter of his commentary, he published it separately, in 1609, under the now famous title of 'Mare Liberum'. The 'Freedom of the Seas', together with the rest of his commentary, was to form much of the basis for the mature treatise he published twenty years later, when war was again raging so fiercely as to threaten the very structure of Europe. 'On the Law of War and Peace' was one of the greatest contributions ever made to the science of international law.

The eighteenth century was not a fortunate one for the Netherlands. From the time of Marlborough, Holland was no longer one of the great powers. The finances of the Republic were exhausted. Following the French Revolution, the army of Pichegru swept over the country in 1794–5, and the 'Batavian Republic' was organized on the French model. As in France, constitution followed constitution, growing progressively less democratic. At the same time the English seized the Dutch colonies, shut up their shipping, and at Camperdown in 1797, destroyed their navy. In 1806 the Batavian Republic was converted into a Monarchy under Louis Napoleon. But his policy was too liberal to please his brother, who therefore incorporated Holland in the French Empire in 1810. Came the defeat of Bonaparte at Leipzig in 1813.

119

It was followed by a general rising in the Netherlands. The Prince of Orange, whose father, William V, had died in exile, hastened back and became 'sovereign prince'. Drafting of a constitution was put in hand.

The following year, 1814, the victorious powers decided to set up as a bulwark against the defeated French, a State uniting all the Netherlands, divided since 1579, together with the Bishopric of Liège and the tiny Duchy of Bouillon. At its head was placed the Prince of Orange, with the title of William I, King of the Netherlands. His share in the German inheritance of the Nassau family was exchanged for Luxemburg, of which, as has been shown, he became Grand Duke.

In this way, after 200 years of struggle for its independent existence, and of striving for the form of government best suited to it, the Dutch Republic became a constitutional monarchy. It still is. The constitution of 1815, with some important amendments has continued in force until now.

Looking at the Dutch constitution as it is today, and examining those principles which are relevant to the present book, it comes as no surprise to read: 'The executive power shall be vested in the King' (Article 56). For this is a continuation of the strong tradition of personal leadership which history reveals to have been always an outstanding characteristic of the Netherlands. Given that history, it is equally not surprising that basically the same principle should be followed in Luxemburg constitutional law (as has been shown) as well as in the breakaway Belgian constitution of 1830 – though this adds the protective rider that it is 'subject to the provisions of the Constitution' that the executive power vests in the King, whilst Luxemburg veers in the opposite direction: 'The Grand Duke *alone* exercises executive power'. In practice, of course, in all three countries executive power is exercised by the Monarch together with his Ministers, or by them on his behalf, but the legal authority for its exercise is the Monarch's. So it is natural to find, also, that 'The King shall constitute ministerial departments. He shall appoint Ministers thereof, and remove them from office at will. . . .' (Article 86), or to find, in Belgium and Luxemburg, that the Monarch appoints and dismisses his Ministers (Article 65 and Article 77, respectively). In Luxemburg, members of the Government are not eligible to be members of the Chamber of Deputies (Article 54), but in Belgium they are (Article 88), while in Holland 'Ministers shall sit in both chambers' of the States–General, but may do so only in an advisory capacity, for they cannot be members, and have no right to vote (Articles 104 and 106). In Holland, the legislative power is 'exercised jointly by the King and the States-General'. (Article 119). This means that draft laws may become approved by either a downward or an upward progression. Either the King may propose legislation for the States-General to approve or, alternatively, 'the States-General have the right to make proposals of law to the King' (Article 126). As has been shown, the same position obtains in Luxemburg.

Over one article in the Dutch Constitution, the shades of Grotius seem to exercise an almost tangible influence: 'The King shall have the supreme direction of foreign relations. He shall promote the development of the international legal order' (Article 58). Since he has the supreme direction of foreign relations, it is natural that agreements with other powers and with international organizations 'must be concluded by or by authority of the King' (Article 60). This part of the Dutch treaty-making process recalls that of the United Kingdom; but from that point on the processes diverge. In Holland, the same article continues,

agreements shall be communicated to the States-General as soon as possible; they shall not be ratified and they shall not enter into force until they have received the approval of the States-General.

This is very similar to what is requisite in Luxemburg, with the difference that in Holland approval does not have to be explicitly expressed by a law (though it may be); approval is reckoned to be given, in specified circumstances, implicitly.

The same article (60) concludes with a provision which in itself can be seen as 'promoting the development of the international legal order'. At any rate it makes a clean sweep of the kind of unwilling obstruction to the internal application of international agreements that the constitutions of other countries may cause. Not only does Holland not have a constitutional court, so that there is no possibility for any judge to refer to it a disputed point of treaty law, but Article 60 debars every judge from himself judging of the constitutionality of agreements. ('The judge shall not be competent to judge of the constitutionality of agreements'.) This provision constitutes the basic reason why the implementation of the European Community treaties, within Holland, has proceeded more smoothly than in most of the other six original members.

But this does not mean that no constitutional check on the internal applicability of treaties exists at all. The check may not be so strong as what was earlier described as the 'moat and drawbridge' protection of the internal body of law in the United Kingdom. Nevertheless, it is there. For, just as all draft internal legislation (whether moving from the King to the States-General, or in the opposite direction) is required to be submitted by the King to the Council of State, so also is the King obliged to 'consult the Council of State on all agreements, with other powers, and organizations based on international law, requiring the approval of the States-General' (Article 84).

A mention of the Dutch Council of State at this juncture may prompt in the reader the question whether this body exercises, besides the advisory function just referred to, the same role of judge of the legality of governmental administrative activity as its namesakes in France, Italy, Belgium and Luxemburg. 'Jurisdiction to determine disputes may be conferred by law on the Council of State, or on a section of that Council', states Article 85 of the Dutch Constitution. This role of the Council of State is, in fact, the same *in kind* as that of its namesakes in the other four countries. But it is not the same *in scope*. For the Council's jurisdiction does not approximate to a general competence to try all disputes between private interests and those of the State – as in varying degree it does in the other countries – but extends only to such disputes as are covered by a law specifically conferring jurisdiction on it.

The reasons for this are historical, and date from 1815. Concerned, at that time, to prevent all return to despotic Government, the Dutch authorities sought the guarantee, not by enlarging or strengthening the role of the Council of State, but in a considerable extension of the jurisdiction of the ordinary law courts. They inscribed this extension in the Constitution of 1815, giving exclusive jurisdiction to the ordinary courts over all disputes concerning property or property rights, as well as over those concerning civil rights and obligations. In identical wording, this provision has become Article 167 of the Constitution that is valid today. But, historically, it was a provision that blocked the way for the time being to the gradual formation of a distinct body of administrative law, in the way that was to constitute so vital a thread in the story of nineteenth-century France.

By the middle of the century, however, leading Dutch legal thinkers were busy drawing attention to this French development. In 1848, when the constitution was under revision, it had been only with the greatest hesitation that the Legislature accepted the Council of State as a permanent feature. But in 1861 the two Chambers of the States-General finally approved a fifth draft law dealing with the Council of State, which, with minor amendments, is still in force today. Preserving its advisory role, the law gave the Council of State an additional 'disputes section' in administrative questions. The function of this section is to advise the Crown in respect of administrative disputes which fall to the Crown for decision. (Somewhat similarly, each judgment of the Judicial Committee of the British Privy Council is, formally, advice to the Queen.) The Crown must, in Holland, determine the dispute, but the number of cases in which it does not accept the opinion of the disputes section of the Council of State is insignificant.* The body of administrative law that the Council of State was free to evolve after 1861 was not, as might have been expected, inspired so much by the French example, as by that of the administrative law being developed by German jurists. This was no doubt partly due to greater familiarity with the language, but the principal reason was the interest and great authority of the leading Dutch Professor of Public Law at Leyden at that period. It was also largely as a result of his influence that in 1877 there was introduced into the constitution the provision already quoted: 'Jurisdiction to determine disputes may be conferred by law on the Council of State, or on a section of that Council.'

*See, generally, van Poelje, Conseiller d'État aux Pays-Bas, in *Le Conseil d'État*, Livre Jubilaire, Paris, Sirey, 1952, pp. 493–8.

Since that time, in other words, there is an alternative. The Council may itself determine a dispute, if a law specifically empowers it to do so, rather than deliver an advisory opinion to assist the Crown to decide.

Enough has been said to indicate that Holland has been fully alert to this modern problem facing all western democracies. Adding inspiration from more than one foreign source to her native legal genius, she appears to be as near as any other country to the best solution possible in the circumstances. Certainly she was in an unrivalled position in regard to the understanding and formulation of the administrative law principles embodied in the three treaties establishing the European Communities.

A reliable system of administrative law is one source of the protection of private interests against those of the State. Individual rights vouchsafed by the National Constitution make up another. The Constitution of the Netherlands enumerates 'equal right to protection of their persons and goods, for all persons who are on the territory of the Kingdom', freedom of the press, the right to petition, the right of association and assembly, free education, and freedom of religion. Other special articles provide for freedom from arrest except on a warrant giving reasons therefor, otherwise than in cases determined by law; security of a person's dwelling against unauthorized entry by another, and the security of letters entrusted to the postal service. Moreover, one article specially provides for a contingency which in the present-day world is of increasingly common occurrence: 'Expropriation for reasons of public utility', states Article 165, 'cannot take place except after a previous declaration by law that public utility necessitates expropriation, and against compensation previously received or previously assured, all in accordance with rules laid down by law'.

Shortly after the Second World War, freed of enemy occupation, and with its constitution restored, the Netherlands stood ready to 'promote the development of the international legal order' not in any mere abstract sense, but by every practical means at her disposal. In full keeping with her history and traditions, it was from The Hague that Mr Winston Churchill (as he then was) launched the European Movement, to sway public opinion over the widest possible area in favour of European unity. The Netherlands became an original member of the Brussels Treaty Organization, the Council of Europe, O.E.E.C., O.E.C.D., Western European Union, and she early ratified the European Convention on Human Rights. Benelux – which, as the name implies, was the fruit of a treaty between Belgium, the Netherlands and Luxemburg – must not be omitted from the list of the internationalizing endeavours of Holland.

In the same period the country became an original member of each of the three European Communities. Recognizing at once the particular exigencies of the treaties establishing them, the Netherlands proceeded at an early date to make alterations in the constitution which would ensure an easy path for the implementation of community law law within the country. Two ammendments. were made, the first in 1953, soon after the setting up of the Coal and Steel Community, and the second in 1956, partly in anticipation, no doubt, of the two further community treaties that were to be signed in 1957.

It has already been pointed out that the courts in the Netherlands cannot be presented with the question of the constitutionality of international treaties into which the country has entered. 'The judge shall not be competent to judge of the constitutionality of international treaties', states Article 60. As a result, the kind of obstacle to community-treaty implementation that has been encountered, particularly in Germany and Italy, cannot exist in the Netherlands. But the Dutch constitution, as amended in the 1950s, smoothes even further the path for the internal implementation of the community treaties. With a provision closely resembling the 1956 amendment to the Luxemburg constitution (Article 49^2 is referred to previously*) it has been put beyond all possible doubt that, for the Netherlands, the transfer to international organizations of the exercise of certain functions of sovereignty is entirely constitutional: '. . . certain powers with respect to legislation, administration and judicial activity may by, or in virtue of, an agreement, be conferred on organizations based on international law,' states Article 67. Moreover, the binding effect 'on anyone' within the Kingdom (of

* [125] p. 110

provisions in international agreements intended to have that effect) is operative from the moment of publication of the agreement in accordance with rules laid down by law (states Article 65). In addition, by Article 66, such provisions of international agreements 'binding on anyone' nullify completely the effect of any internal legal requirements that are incompatible with them – whether or not the internal legal requirements are introduced before or after publication of the international provisions. And, finally to smooth the path, 'decisions made by organizations based on international law' (such as those of the Community institutions) are made, by Article 67, to take precisely the same precedence over internal law as do the provisions of international agreements themselves, in the way just described. (The procedure for implementing, in the Netherlands, the subsidiary legislation of the Communities is less complicated than in some other member States. Much can be done by the tacit approval of the States-General to laws implementing community regulations, for example. Or the Crown, or a ministry, may have power, as in other countries, to issue administrative regulations having the force of law [for example, in export–import matters].)

All this, it must be said, constitutes in very marked fashion 'promotion of the development of the international legal order'. To complete this particular aspect of the legal portrait of Holland, it should be added that the constitution even makes provision for cases of inconsistency between itself and an international treaty which it is the intention to ratify: 'If the development of the international legal order requires this, the contents of an (international) agreement may deviate from certain provisions of the constitution' (Article 63). For such an agreement, approval must be by a two thirds majority of the votes cast in each of the two chambers of the States-General.

In this connexion, one matter has given the States-General reason to pause. As will be explained in a later chapter, the role of the 'European Parliament' within the framework of the Communities is not that of a day-to-day legislative body. There is therefore no community body, analogous to itself, to which the Dutch Parliament could willingly conceive its legislative powers as being at least partially transferred. So long as that is the situation, it has preferred to reserve *to itself* the right to approve international agreements that are contemplated in pursuance of the E.E.C. and Euratom Treaties. Accordingly, it amended the draft Dutch laws ratifying these two treaties so as to reserve its position in that respect. Association agreements between the E.E.C. and non-member States, for example, must therefore have the approval of the Dutch Parliament – not simply that of the Dutch Government, to which, in any event, Parliament has not delegated any specific powers to discharge obligations under community law.

4

The Community's Constitution

IN the last chapter, an inkling was given of the methods by which rules and orders emanating from the European Communities ('Regulations', 'Directives', 'Decisions') gain entry into the internal legal systems of each of the member States, there to affect the lives of individuals. In practice it is mainly indirectly that individuals are likely to feel the effects. These will permeate through to them as associations of individuals – such as trading companies, industrial undertakings, associations of producers or sellers of agricultural produce, etc. – find their activities conditioned by legal requirements coming from this new source. These legal requirements are, in fact, rules and orders.

But, technically, they are called 'Regulations' or 'Decisions' when their effect on such associations (or on individuals) does not require the intervention of the member State to which such associations (or individuals) belong. When the lives of individuals or their associations can only be affected by such intervention on the part of their own member State, the legal requirement from which this result will follow will be a 'Directive' – which is really an order to a member State, from the Community, to take whatever measures the State may consider necessary to achieve the object which the Community defines in the directive.

The fact that regulations and decisions may be addressed by the Community directly to associations of individuals and to individuals themselves, is yet another example of the phenomenon to which attention was drawn in a reference to Magna Carta at the very beginning of this book. For the possibility of making such enforceable regulations and decisions expresses, as a matter of law, the shape of the Order they represent. Here is a new type of law and order, a new form of human grouping.*The slow historical

*In a remarkable judgment of 18 October 1967, the German Federal Constitutional Court highlighted a number of the characteristic features of a 'Community': Its regulations, not being acts of the German public author-

progression of human society in Europe to the nation State of modern times is taking a new turn. The territorial boundaries of States have become intolerably irksome or out of date for certain of the activities of men. Freedom of trade, of movement, of selection of a place in which to live and work, or to which to move financial capital, all these are economic or social requirements and ambitions which, since the Second World War, have in Europe made men increasingly chafe at national frontiers. It is to eliminate them by progressive stages, so far as they run counter to these requirements and ambitions, that the European Communities exist – though that is by no means their only purpose. The motive force that led to their creation was not only the human instinct for self-fulfilment, but the instinct for self-preservation, with which this book began; and the ultimate purposes of the Communities are openly stated to be political.

This new form of human grouping brings men into a legal relationship, towards each other as well as towards the new central authority, that transcends certain aspects of their legal relationship to the State of which they are nationals, or in which they reside. But it is a relationship that they entered into through the instrumentality of their respective States. Using the State legal equipment of sovereignty and independence, the equipment of treaty-making procedure, and the constitutional legal machinery for the ratification and implementation of the treaty so made, men took not only themselves into community grouping, but the State to which they belonged as well. Certain of the functions of the internal sovereignty of States were pooled in order to be exercised by the central power in the Community; and the

---

ity, could not be challenged as to their constitutionality in German law (Law of the Federal Constitutional Court, Article 90); the legal nature of the Communities was such that they were neither States nor Confederations of States, but inter-State institutions within the meaning of Article 24 of the Basic Law: as to the sovereign rights of the Communities, these constituted a new sovereign power, autonomous and independent, so that their acts were directly applicable without approval or ratification by member States; the member States had no power to abrogate community acts; community law was an original and autonomous legal order, being neither international law nor internal law, and it represented a system of legal protection and security to be distinguished from the internal legal system of a member State.

complete freedom of States to exercise external sovereignty in concluding treaties with other States, not members of the Community, was subjected to limitations in the interest of the Community. And at the outset, as the first community treaty was drafted, the realization that here – at least in embryo – was a new form of human grouping unparalleled in the world, was given point to, and accentuated, by the specific agreement of the member States that disputes between them in respect of this particular treaty should not be referred to the international Court of Justice at The Hague – the normally accepted forum for inter-State disputes. If the new treaty should give rise to disputes between States, they would be taken to the Community's own Court of Justice.

The question of how power or authority in the Community was to be exercised, was of course not left (as in earlier human groupings) for later struggles to decide. As far as men's imagination could anticipate the situations in which its exercise would be required, and with the use of existing experience of constitutional law, the answer came ready made off the drawing board, so to speak, on which the community treaty was prepared for the signatures of the would-be member States. The three forms that all exercise of governmental authority may take – executive, legislative and judicial – were each assigned their respective roles by the treaty. They were in fact institutionalized, since, in order positively to assign these roles, the treaty created the institutions or bodies who were to exercise each of them. In the relationship of the community institutions to each other, to the member States, and to the individuals or associations of individuals wi‘hin the member States, resides the essence of the constitutional law of the Communities. Since the treaties themselves define these relationships, it is the treaties that are the written constitution of the Communities, and the Communities thus have a constitution that they were born with.

The treaties did more than bring the Communities into being, and lay down the constitution by which their operations were to be governed. The matter was not left there, though conceivably it could have been. Instead, each treaty proceeded to lay down a programme of action for the Community to which it gave birth, in terms ranging from the specific to the general. To do this was an act of legislation, performed collectively by the six States that signed and ratified the treaties. (Indeed. 'international legislation' is the convenient expression used by lawyers for treaties of this and similar kinds.) The Communities thus came into existence not only with a constitution to govern the method or manner of their operations, but also with laws to govern the actual nature and content of these operations – as if a pre-natal Legislature, intrinsic to them in their embryonic state, had been at work.

Since the major part, if not all, of the legislative work, strictly so-called, had been done for the Communities before they came into existence, there was clearly less need for the treaty makers to provide for a Legislature, as an institution of each Community, having the prominent day-to-day role which characterizes the Legislatures of individual democratic States. What, in the event, they did provide for, was a parliamentary Assembly having 'advisory and supervisory powers' (as they were defined in Article 137 of the E.E.C. Treaty), rather than powers that are legislative in the usual sense. The Assembly advises the Council of Ministers. It, or its members, may ask questions of the Commission (an executive institution of the Community) by whom oral or written answers must be provided. It does not, however, meet in regular session, but usually six to eight times a year. An extraordinary session may be demanded by a majority of its members (or of the Commission or of the Council). Its most important power enables it by a vote of censure to force the collective resignation of the members of the Commission. This is a power it is perhaps unlikely to use, but it is nevertheless a form of ultimate control of the Executive by the Assembly. Any more immediate control, as distinct from supervision, is absent. There is nothing resembling the immediate responsibility of the Executive to Parliament, as in the British Constitution.

In one aspect of the community system there does, however, exist a similarity. The British Parliament now frequently enacts a Statute, the detailed implementation of which it leaves to the Executive (that is, to the appropriate Minister or his department). The Executive, to implement the Statute, makes regulations or orders, or conducts inquiries. The rules or orders thus made have, as their name betokens, a primarily legislative character. They are referred to as 'delegated legislation', since Parliament, by the Statute, has delegated its legislative power to the Executive so that it may make rules and orders. In the Communities, the legislative programme embodied in the treaties resembles somewhat a Statute. The community Executive implements the programme by making rules or orders (Regulations, Decisions, Directives). These, equally, are primarily legislative in character, though made by the Executive, and it appears likely that in Britain they will come to be collectively referred to as the Community's 'subsidiary legislation'. There is a further similarity. In the inquiries conducted by the Executive in Britain in implementing a Statute there is likely to be a strong judicial or at least quasi-judicial element, and the same is true of some of the activities of the Community. Although such activities there result in what are referred to as 'decisions', which is technically a designation of executive acts, they may none the less be judicial in essence.

The existence of delegated legislation in Britain appears to be an unavoidable necessity in modern circumstances.* Nevertheless, safeguards are available against its abuse. There are three types of safeguard: Parliamentary, Political and Judicial. In matters of overall national importance, a Statute that enables delegated legislation to be made, now frequently requires it to be 'laid before' Parliament. This 'laying before' may mean, according to what the Statute stipulates, that an affirmative resolution of either or both Houses of Parliament is required before the delegated legislation comes into force, or that it may be the subject of a negative vote in Parliament that would prevent it coming into force. Further parliamentary safeguards lie in the power of members of either House to ask questions concerning delegated legislation, to call for a debate, or even to move the censure of the government.

There is some degree of political safeguard when the enabling Statute provides that the Minister concerned should consult interested bodies or an advisory committee before issuing regulations.

*See the discussion of this matter in Chapter 3, pp. 46f.

The essence of the judicial safeguard in Britain against delegated legislation lies in the power of the court to nullify delegated legislation in any case where it is not in accordance with the provisions of the enabling Statute, or where it goes beyond the powers conferred by it. In either of these events the delegated legislation is declared by the court to be 'ultra vires' – that is 'exceeding the powers' conferred by the enabling Statute.

In this concept of 'exceeding the powers', which is the dominant concept in British administrative law, can be seen a joining of hands with the community system. For the identical concept of 'excès de pouvoir', taken from French administrative law, for embodiment in that of the Community, provides the basis for the four specific grounds on which a regulation, directive or decision may be annulled by the Community Court of Justice. These four specific grounds (the same as those evolved in the case law of the French Conseil d'État, from which they have been taken) are set out in the community treaties with indications of the circumstances in which they may be invoked. The parties that may invoke them before the Community Court of Justice, are member States or private parties (who, in practice, are most likely to be companies, or industrial or agricultural undertakings, but may be individuals). Together, these grounds represent a comprehensive legal protection against abuse of executive power in the Community, for they are constituted by (i) lack of powers; (ii) violations of basic procedural rules; (iii) infringement of the treaty or of any rule of law relating to its implementation; and (iv) misuse of powers (which means the using of a power, by the Executive, for a purpose other than that for which the power was conferred upon it). Since they are prescribed by the treaties themselves, they constitute a *legislative* provision of instruments employable by the Judiciary. 'Ultra vires', in the British system, is not a legislative provision but an instrument moulded by the Judiciary itself in the traditional way. 'Excès de pouvoir' was originally moulded in a similar way by the Judiciary of the French Conseil d'État – and appears to have reached a fuller degree of perfection than the British counterpart.

In the Communities, then, judicial safeguards against the abuse of power by the Executive are at least as complete as they are in Britain, if not more so. What have been referred to above as political safeguards also exist in the Communities, for there is frequently a treaty requirement that the Executive shall consult advisory bodies before action. Moreover, there is integrated into the work of the Commission (and also into that of the Council), the regular advice of a group of permanent and highly qualified legal consultants.

On the other hand, the community equivalents of British parliamentary safeguards are much weaker. There is no 'laying before'; indeed, in the nature of things, there cannot be, because the Assembly is not regularly in session. It is true that the Assembly or its members may question the Commission, and in the last resort compel its resignation, but the treaties have allowed the Executive to cut loose from regular legislative control, and this is the ground upon which a certain body of opinion in continental Europe questions the adequacy of the community constitutional structure. As has been shown in the previous chapter, this questioning has on occasion been translated, particularly in Germany, into arguments before national courts aiming to invalidate community measures or to hinder their execution. The arguments have been directed at showing the unconstitutionality of community procedures judged by the standards of the national constitution.

As a matter of fact, when the E.E.C. and Euratom Treaties were being drafted in 1956, there had been considerable support for inserting the provision that community regulations should not be issued unless their compatibility with the constitutions of member States had first been ensured. But the opposite view prevailed, because of the great difficulty that the community institutions would experience, if on the occasion of each regulation they had to assess its compatibility with six different sets of constitutional requirements.

Continental anxieties on this score were well summarized by Professor A. de Vreese of the College of Europe at Bruges, speaking in April 1965:

When in some of our countries, constitutional objections are raised against the exercise of powers that are in substance legislative by a community body that is formally executive; when it is seen that the national legislative power is reluctant to entrust the execution of community law to a national executive authority; when our national courts are somewhat non-plussed when asked to give pre-eminence over the national law to a community regulation emanating from a community executive, can this not be traced back in every case to the lack – within the community order – of any real democratic control on the part of a legislative Assembly?

The Assembly, or 'European Parliament' as it is now called, was brought into being by the treaties with a membership of 142 delegates, nominated in specified proportions by, and from the members of, the Parliaments of the member States. The treaties envisage, at a later stage, elections to membership 'by direct universal suffrage in accordance with a uniform procedure in all member States'. It cannot therefore be said that its composition is not democratically conceived. What is criticized, both outside the Parliament and within it, is the incompleteness of its democratic control over the day-to-day life of the Communities.

This factor, or weakness, constitutes a problem that could be more acute in the future than it is at present. Admittedly, law-making activity by a community body that is executive accords ill with any theory of the strict separation of powers. But it is not an unfamiliar phenomenon in the internal systems of the individual member States, as has been shown. Moreover, the subsidiary legislation so made can only be in execution of an internationally agreed economic and social programme laid down in advance in the treaties; the Executive is not cast loose, by the legislation of the treaties, to enact anything it pleases. The Communities' Court of Justice has ample powers to ensure that this agreed programme is not exceeded, and, if that were not enough guarantee, there are the other safeguards just mentioned. It is within those limits that the problem presents itself for the time being.

For the time being the prescribed programme is economic and social. But the ultimate objective of the Communities is political. It is expressed in the opening words of the E.E.C. Treaty, as a determination 'to establish the foundations of an ever closer union among the European peoples'. This is what Dr Hallstein, when President of the Commission, meant when he said: 'We are not in business, we are in politics.' This is the context in which the constitutional problem of democratic parliamentary control would become more acute. It is the context which gives point to the comment in paragraph XLII of the 10th Report (1967) of the E.E.C. Commission:

In the Commission's eyes, the Community has always been a political union in the economic and social fields. Its institutions – the Parliament, the Council, the Commission, – are political institutions. If further proof of the Community's political character were needed, it would be found in the clearly expressed will of the peoples of the six countries and their Governments to maintain and advance the Community despite the most severe strains and difficulties. The extension beyond the economic and social spheres of those areas where 'ever closer union' of the peoples of Europe is being achieved is, if not the corollary, at any rate a natural extension of the existing Communities. The Commission has always taken an interest in efforts to extend the Community. It must repeat that initiatives of this kind succeed only if they lead to the establishment of a European constitutional order in the other spheres, an order which, whatever its structure, would include institutions capable of guiding a destiny which from now on is shared.

From this glimpse of trends for the future, there must now be a return to complete the picture of the present. Mention has been made of the role of the Community Judiciary in controlling the legality of the exercise of its powers by the Community Executive. It must be clear that the importance of that judicial role is enhanced all the more by the weakness of community parliamentary control of the Executive – though Judiciary and Parliament are never an exact substitute one for the other.

The importance of this aspect of its jurisdiction is also reflected in the high proportion of cases concerned with it that the Communities' Court of Justice has been called upon to decide. But besides keeping the action of the community Executives within the law, the court has also to award compensation for damages caused by community institutions. These two types of activity together make up the first of the four main functions of the Court – the judicial control of the community institutions.

This particular aspect of its jurisdiction (which until latterly has been by far the most important) is unlikely to continue to be so. The reason may be put quite simply. Judicial control of the executive power is particularly important in the Coal and Steel Community, because that treaty introduced a system of *direct* administration of specific industries, by the executive power in the Community, in accordance with a specific programme of economic action which the treaty also laid down. Consequently, the high proportion of administrative law cases before the court from 1954 to 1959 were proceedings brought by industrial undertakings in the Coal or Steel sector of the economy, aiming to annul or to mitigate the effects of decisions of the Community Executive that the undertakings were displeased with. By contrast, the two later treaties (E.E.C. and Euratom) introduced a system not of *direct* but of *indirect* administration by the Community Executive, of a programme of economic action that, essentially, could not be specific, since it embraces all economic activity – industrial, agricultural, and the servicing activities whose fruits or earnings are commonly referred to in Britain as 'invisibles'. As a result, in implementing these later treaties, the administrative action of the community Executives had to be much more indirect, taking effect through the intermediary of the member States. Consequently, it is in the national courts that the implementation of these later treaties comes more frequently to be challenged. Where this occurs, any doubt that arises in the national court as to the correct interpretation of the treaty, for example, or as to the validity or interpretation of acts of the institutions of the Community, may be referred to the Communities' Court of Justice for a ruling (and *must* be so referred by a national court from which in the national system no appeal lies to a higher court). The giving of preliminary rulings in this way is a second aspect of the court's jurisdiction, which since about 1961 has been assuming steadily increasing importance. In exercising it, the court may be seen not only as seeking to ensure the uniform application of community law throughout the Community, but also as the custodian of the constitution of the Community (as well as the interpreter of its subsidiary legislation).

But the full role of the court is wider still. It is defined by the treaties as 'ensuring that the law is observed in the interpretation and implementation of the treaties.' This gives it a very wide range of action indeed, and two further main functions become apparent: (1) to ensure that the treaties are also correctly implemented by the member States and by other persons; and (2) to exercise certain powers of a constitutional nature.

Among the last-named powers a good example is provided by Article 95 of the Coal and Steel Community Treaty. This article permits the provisions of the treaty to be amended, in certain circumstances, by an internal procedure of the Community not requiring the participation of the governments or parliaments of the six member States. But before the internal procedure can in fact effect a revision of the treaty in the way desired, the Court of Justice must express the opinion that the circumstances requiring the revision really do exist. Moreover, the court must also be of the opinion that the proposed amendments are genuinely in conformity with the general principles laid down in the introductory part of the treaty itself.

The function listed above as (1) is the result of the fact that responsibility for applying the treaties does not lie only with the community institutions – though they provide the driving force for much of the process. The treaties also impose positive or negative obligations on the member States and on other persons: the member States are *not allowed*, for example, to grant aids or subsidies, and individuals and companies *are obliged* to comply with the free competition rules of the treaties. A member State which fails to fulfil such treaty obligations may be brought before the community Court of Justice by another member State or a community institution; a company or an individual may appeal to the court against a fine imposed for failure to comply with the free competition rules.

In short, whatever aspect of community law is involved the Communities' Court of Justice is the final arbiter of it. The crisscross pattern of relationships between community institutions, member States, and persons that are their nationals or reside in their territory, characterizes this new form of human grouping. It also makes possible a great variety of situations in which institutions, States and other persons may find themselves at legal odds before the Court. The four main functions which it exercises have been described only in the barest outline, and others have been left out of the account.

The reader who recalls, early in this book, the description of judicial independence, and of its great importance, in the purely national setting of the United Kingdom, will appreciate that it is no less important in this criss-cross pattern of community relationships. So it is a matter of the deepest significance that the treaties place the Court of Justice in a position of complete independence, not only of the member States, but also of the community institutions, both executive and parliamentary.

The judges of the Court are appointed by mutual agreement between the governments of member States, and 'chosen from persons whose independence can be fully guaranteed and who fulfil the conditions required for the exercise of the highest judicial functions in their respective countries or who are legal experts of universally recognized and outstanding ability'. On assuming office, they have a duty to serve only the interests of the Communities, disregarding the particular interests of the nation to which they belong – in the same way as the judges of the International Court of Justice at The Hague – the World Court – act independently of their respective countries of national origin. Judges, however, are no less human than other men. While their known individual character, and the methods of working of the Communities' Court, are sufficient guarantee against conscious regard to purely national interest, there is nevertheless some risk that individual judges may unconsciously tend to reason primarily along the lines with which their lifetime training and experience in a purely national system of law has made them most familiar. Any such tendency is not diminished by the fact that the law of the Communities, and the procedures of the court, are in some measure a synthesis of comparable legal concepts rooted in the different national traditions. Consequently, had there not been provision for judgments to be based on the view of a majority of the judges – and for minority views not to be made public – there might have been detectable, for example, some fairly consistent divergence between the Latin and the Germanic traditions of law in the work of the Communities' Court. Instead, the court is evolving a body of case law unfettered in any way by national traditions, though owing something to them. The result is a consensus transcending national inspiration, as are the Communities to which it applies.

From all that has gone before in this chapter the greater part of the overall picture emerges of the system of legal security provided by the treaties for the Communities. The more they advance in the programmes assigned to them, the more will that system be asserted and tested. At the same time, economic and social life in the member States will increasingly reveal the influence of the Communities' programmes in those fields. But in launching the Communities upon these programmes, and establishing, independently of the member States, a system of legal security for them, the treaties did not turn their backs on economic circumstances within the individual member States. How could they?

The economic consequences of projecting a system on to a wider territorial area than that of any single member State would necessarily be superimposed on the economic circumstances existing within them. It is therefore not only positive measures of legal security for the operation of the Communities that the treaties seek to provide, but also negative measures, aimed at ensuring that economic circumstances in the member States shall not be adversely effected. Thus the E.E.C. Treaty: 'This treaty shall in no way prejudice existing systems and incidents of ownerships' (Article 222); and

The provisions of this treaty shall not adversely affect the following rules: (a) no member State shall be obliged to supply information the disclosure of which it considers contrary to the essential interest of its security; (b) Any member State may take whatever measures it considers necessary for the protection of the essential interests of its security, and which are connected with the production of or trade in arms, munitions and war material; such measures shall, however, not adversely affect conditions of competition in the Common Market in the case of products which are not intended for specifically military purposes (Article 223).

Of the four forms of security – legal, physical, economic and social – which a free society requires if it is to flourish, two find reflection in these articles: the physical or defensive, and, so far as private rights are concerned, the economic.

Economic security, in a general or public sense, is the concern of Article 226:

> If, during the transitional period, serious difficulties, which might persist, arise in one sector of the economy, or if there are difficulties which may result in a region suffering grave economic hardship, a member State may request authority to take protective measures in order to rectify the position and adapt the sector concerned to the economy of the Common Market.

It is the Commission of the Community which determines what protective measures are necessary. These may include derogations from the rules of the treaty.

So much by way of indication of negative measures for protection of States, their nationals and residents. The picture of the system of legal security of the Communities, safeguarding the present while conditioning the future in terms of the programme agreed in the treaties, is thereby completed. It remains, in this chapter, to take a quick look at the motive power which impels the Communities on their evolutionary course, and at the freedoms and liberties to which individuals become legally entitled in the new form of human grouping thereby taking shape.

The motive power in the (later) Communities, as is well known, is provided by the Commission in conjunction with the Council of Ministers. Since 1967 a single Commission of fourteen members has taken on the work of the three bodies that formerly existed, that is, the Commissions of E.E.C. and Euratom and the High Authority of the E.C.S.C. It is laid down by the treaties that

> the members of the Commission shall perform their duties in complete independence, in the general interest of the Communities. In the performance of their duties, they shall neither seek nor take instructions from any Government or other body.

Like the judges of the Communities' Court, the members of the Commission serve only the interests of the new human groupings which the Communities constitute. They owe no duty to, and must avoid being influenced by, the member States of which they are respectively the nationals. With regard to the Economic Community their task is defined as follows:

In order to ensure that the Common Market works efficiently and develops satisfactorily, the Commission shall: ensure that the provisions of this treaty and the measures taken by the Institutions by virtue of this treaty are carried out: formulate recommendations or give opinions on matters within the scope of this Treaty, if it expressly so provides or if the Commission considers this necessary: have power to take decisions and, in the circumstances provided for in this Treaty, participate in the shaping of measures taken by the Council and the [Parliamentary] Assembly: exercise the powers conferred on it by the Council to ensure effect being given to rules laid down by the latter (E.E.C. Article 155).

The Council of Ministers has seventeen members (France, Germany and Italy provide four each. Belgium and the Netherlands two each, Luxemburg one.) In exceptional matters, such as the application for admission to the Community by a European State, the treaty requires the Council to decide by a unanimous vote. But in the normal way its resolutions may be passed by a majority of twelve votes in favour (any twelve, in a vote on a proposal of the Commission; twelve votes cast by at least four members in all other cases). The Council 'disposes of a power of decision'. In other words it is an executive Institution, and may issue regulations, directives and decisions in the technical sense described earlier in this chapter for the particular needs of community development. In general, as regards E.E.C., its work is defined as follows:

To ensure the achievement of the objectives laid down in this Treaty, and in accordance with the provisions thereof, the Council shall ensure that the economic policies of the member States are coordinated.

The coordination of economic policies is one method – establishing the Common Market is the other – by which the E.E.C. Treaty requires the Community to fulfil its task. That task is 'to promote throughout the Community a harmonious development of economic activities, a continuous and balanced expansion, an increased stability, an accelerated raising of the standard of living and closer relations between its member States' (E.E.C. Article 2).

An increased enjoyment of the good things of life made possible by economic stability and expansion is, in human and material terms, the aim. The good things of life are, however, not only the material ones, though these may be the springboard making it possible for human beings to attain to the others. All of them are the fruits of the free way of life.

Economic stability and expansion, material prosperity, the fruits of the free way of life – the Communities have a concern for them all, and that concern is writ large in the treaties. Eliminate economic restrictions, says the E.E.C. Treaty. Remove customs duties and quantitative restrictions on the import and export of goods.* Eliminate distortions of free competition. Abolish obstacles to the free movement of persons, services and capital. Inaugurate common policies for agriculture and for transport. Adopt procedures permitting the coordination of the economic policies of member States and the correction of instability in their balances of payments. Create a Social Fund in order to improve the possibilities of employment for workers and to contribute to the raising of their standard of living. Maintain, through the Commission, all appropriate relations with the organs of the United Nations, their specialized Agencies and the General Agreement on Tariffs and Trade. Cooperate with the Council of Europe wherever desirable. Establish close co-operation with O.E.E.C. (now O.E.C.D.). Do not bar the existence or development of regional unions between Belgium and Luxemburg, and between Belgium, Luxemburg and the Netherlands ('Benelux') where these unions aim at purposes additional to those of the community treaties. Do not interfere with the rights and obligations arising from agreements concluded before the Community was established, by member States with States who have not become members, unless the agreements are incompatible with the Community. Remove obstructions, and build for a fuller life for human beings. But neither interfere with nor destroy anything that does not obstruct this purpose.

Since that is the concept inspiring the Communities, it furnishes the answer to any mistaken belief that membership of the Communities implies the wholesale overthrow of the ordinary law by which the citizens of a would-be member State are governed.

*On 1 July 1968 the Customs Union was fully established, 18 months before the Schedule laid down in the E.E.C.Treaty.

On the contrary, for the purposes of the Economic Community, no more is required than 'the approximation of the respective national laws of member States *to the extent required for the Common Market to function in an orderly manner*' (emphasis added by present author). It is consequently only on the periphery of the ordinary private law of member States that direct changes require to be made.

But as against each member State the private rights of persons subject to its jurisdiction may well be buttressed – or, indeed, newly created – as a direct result of a community treaty, that is to say, without the positive intervention of either the community executive power, or of the legislative or executive power of the member State. For example, the Communities' Court of Justice has ruled that Article 95 of the E.E.C. Treaty, which prohibits fiscal discrimination by member States, has thereby conferred on their nationals the right to be protected against such discrimination.* This is a right, moreover, which they may enforce in the national courts, just as they may enforce any right conferred on them by the internal law of the State to which they are subject. The reader may recognize in this new phenomenon something broadly comparable to the operation of the European Convention on Human Rights: for in that case also, an inter-State agreement produced direct effects on individual rights within a member State. For the more immediate argument, however, the importance of this effect of Article 95 of the E.E.C. Treaty (and of others similar to it) is that it demonstrates one essential aspect of the legal nature of the Communities: these are not merely communities of States, but of States and individuals (or their associations) alike.

The criminal law of each member State is left untouched by the community treaties. Also unaffected are the constitutional rights and obligations of citizens and the political allegiance they owe There is, of course, no effect on the legal advantages available to the citizens of those countries which have ratified such international agreements as the European Convention on Human Rights. The ordinary national law relating to restrictive practices by business, or to taxation, or to exchange control – this is the

*See the case before the German Bundesfinanzhof, outlined on p. 82.

kind of peripheral law, if it may be so called, in which direct changes will be necessary. Similarly, in the field of administrative regulation – covering, for example, such matters as preservatives in foodstuffs, or weight-measuring instruments, and so on – some approximation to a unified system is being imposed by community authority.

'Close collaboration' between member States in the social field – that is, something less than *approximation* of their respective laws – is enjoined by the E.E.C. Treaty (Article 118). It is the Commission's task to promote it, particularly in the fields of employment, labour legislation and working conditions, elementary and advanced vocational training, social security, protection against occupational accidents and diseases, industrial hygiene, trade union legislation and collective negotiations between employers and workers. Labour law – the law covering trade unions and collective bargaining – thus remains as one example within the province of member States. The community treaties do not legislate in this field, or in the others contained in the list just given. There is thus no 'body' of community law, properly so called, in these fields, and no legislative base upon which the Communities' Court of Justice could, by interpretation of the treaties, develop a case law. Only indirectly, through the collaboration of member States, will a harmonized system take full effect over all the territory within the Community. When that point is reached, it might loosely be described as community law – but it will not be law over which the community has direct legislative or judicial control, unless the treaties are amended with that intent.

Accordingly, the British Trades Union Congress, in its review 'Britain and the E.E.C.', was able to come to the following considered opinion:

If harmonization does not mean that different systems are all to be made identical, but merely requires the elimination of contradictions and differences which are unjustified by particular requirements or differences in social structure, then the commitment under Article 118 would not impose obligations which would be a threat to the prevailing British system of social security. There can be little doubt that Commission-sponsored studies under Article 118 have helped to spread information amongst the Six of each other's strengths and weaknesses in the field of social security, and this has, in turn, set in train a process of unspectacular imitation of the best practices.

By contrast, member States are not merely enjoined but *obliged* by the E.E.C. Treaty to maintain the principle of equal pay for equal work as between men and women, and to maintain paid holiday schemes on a basis equivalent to that existing on ratification of the treaty. These matters are thus the direct subject of community law, not of mere collaboration between states. They form a part of the treaty legislation, over the interpretation and application of which the Communities' Court has jurisdiction.

Earlier in this book the Communities were referred to as a new form of human society in embryo. From what has so far been said in this chapter the reader may well have concluded that that human society is already well advanced beyond the embryonic stage. So many of the features that characterize a coherent and cohesive society are clearly already in existence. A fundamental law or constitution; interacting governmental institutions with clearly defined powers; a clear and still clarifying relationship between individuals (or their associations) on the one hand, and the institutions and constitution of the Communities on the other; in consequence, a measure of change in the legal relationship between individuals (or their associations) and the member States of which they are nationals or residents; in consequence, too, a measure of change in the traditional legal form of relationships between the member States themselves, as well as with their own nationals and residents – and those of other member States.

In other words, a new legal order is in existence: that of the Communities. It is a legal order which is completely autonomous. That is to say, it is nourished and developed out of sources that are exclusively community sources, upon the basis of the constitution with which each Community was provided by the treaty. No law-making authority other than those of the Communities themselves can make community law. And community law stands as a legal order quite distinct from those of community member States, though it is within these States, in juxtaposition to and interaction with their respective internal legal orders, that it falls to be applied.

Here indeed is a living organism, a new form of society. Neither a Nation, nor a State, nevertheless a human grouping, with features reminiscent of its parentage. In a word – a legal word – a 'person'. 'The Community shall have legal personality', states each treaty. As a legal person, it may and does – acting through its representative Institutions – make contracts (witness the Loan Agreements, for example, of E.C.S.C.); take leases or acquire freeholds of property (as in Luxemburg and Brussels, or in the capital cities of non-member States where it maintains permanent delegations); sue or be sued in its own name in the ordinary courts. It can, in fact, do most things that a State can do. But though it can even negotiate treaties with non-member States or international organizations, the final conclusion of a treaty will normally require the participation, by their signature and ratification, of its member States jointly with the Community. For if that participation were not forthcoming, a treaty made with the Community would be subject to the defect that certain of its provisions might fail to be carried out, if they were beyond the powers of the Community positively to enforce upon its member States. Conversely, a non-member State, or an international organization, that enters into a treaty with a Community may need (or at least wish) to rely – for the ultimate legal sanction for due performance of the treaty – upon adherence to the treaty by the member States of which the Community is in some respect a legal dependent. One of the earliest treaties made with a non-member State as one party, and, as the other party, the Community jointly with its member States, was the Treaty of Association between the U.K. and the European Coal and Steel Community which came into force in September 1955.

So, in its external dealings, as well as in its own internal affairs, the Community reveals itself as a new concept. Influential in world affairs though each Community is increasingly becoming, enjoying in large measure an independent existence, it remains, in law, legally dependent upon its member States. It is not fully sovereign, as is a State. At least, not at present. Though 'the

Community shall have legal personality', that personality does not appear as yet to be a fully-fledged international legal personality.

5

Political Aspects

THIS chapter begins with what may appear to be a short digression from the theme of the legal nature of the Communities, which the discussion has now reached. But the brief treatment of E.F.T.A. which now follows serves not only to complete the general picture so far given of the organizations working towards the unification of Europe, but also as a focal point for comparison with the legal nature of the Communities, and as an introduction to what lies ahead for them.

By contrast with the European Communities, the arrangement made by the countries often referred to as the 'Outer Seven' did not bring into existence a legal 'person'. The European Free Trade Area (E.F.T.A.) was of course brought into being by a treaty signed and ratified by its member States. It was not, however, a treaty of integration but one of cooperation – albeit a treaty which conferred limited powers of enforcement by the Council it established of that Council's own recommendations, and thus followed the pattern of some of the other treaties of cooperation discussed in Chapter 2. Unlike the Communities, and, indeed, unlike the results of some of the other treaties of cooperation, E.F.T.A. was born out of no more than a 'commercial reflex'. For when it became clear that a broad free-trade system comprising all the eighteen then members of O.E.E.C. was unattainable, the Outer Seven, thrown back upon themselves, decided no more than to attempt (by progressively abolishing tariffs between themselves, without introducing a common external tariff) to increase trade among themselves, in order to compensate for any loss of trade in the markets of the Communities of which they were not members, and in order to place themselves in a stronger position to bargain with the six Community countries, whenever negotiations for a broad free-trade system should be renewed.

For these purposes, it was not necessary to create a legal

person or an organization even remotely resembling the Communities. The aims of E.F.T.A. were transitory, not permanent and evolutionary. A minimum of institutional machinery was needed, and of constitutional framework there is very little, unless the power of the Council (composed of government representatives) is so regarded. The Council may hear complaints of member governments, recommend remedies and authorize suspension of benefits against any member government which refuses to comply with a recommendation. In establishing in 1960 this slender framework, the Outer Seven (Denmark, Norway, Sweden, Austria, Switzerland, Portugal and the United Kingdom) sought to achieve their admittedly limited objectives with the minimum of obligation, and the minimum limitation on their national economic policies.

E.F.T.A. could be established without pause for concern at the inclusion of neutral states, such as Austria and Switzerland, within its membership. For it had no defined long-term political objectives such as were making the European Economic Community – at about the same time – ask itself, for example, whether a neutral State could conscientiously adhere to the Treaty of Rome. As living organisms, legal persons, with a political purpose, this was, of course, not the only question that the Communities were bound to ask themselves. What of States that did not share this purpose? Should they be admitted to participate in the commercial benefits of the Communities in a degree that the common external tariff, for one thing, would deny to such countries as the U.S.A. and the U.K.? Should a non-democratic country be permitted to become a member of the Communities? Would a developing country have the economic strength to do so? And, so far as the admission of neutrals was concerned, should there be any difference of treatment between a country like Switzerland, with her long-standing tradition of neutrality by choice, and Austria, the most significant part of whose neutrality, in the context of the question, was the requirement of her treaty with Russia that she might not be drawn into close association with Germany?

Point was given to all these and other questions, in 1961 by the applications for community membership made by Denmark and

Eire (as well as by the U.K.), by the application by Spain in February 1962 for association and possible future membership, and by Austria, Sweden and Switzerland seeking, at about the same time, some form of association with the Economic Community in the hope of achieving a single European market. For the Communities, being a person was bringing the inevitable problems of how to deal with other persons!

But being a person also meant, for each Community, forming, realizing and strengthening its own character. Should not the Economic Community, for example, tangibly and early represent a common commercial policy of its member States? And an energy policy, a transport policy, a monetary policy, and so on? What was the road forward from customs union to a thorough-going economic union?

All these matters and questions had been gradually finding their way towards clarification when, in 1967, a further note of urgency was added to them, not merely by the simultaneously renewed applications of the U.K., Eire and Denmark for community membership. For Norway also (24 July) requested negotiations for full membership, and two days later, in the words of *European Community*,* 'Sweden expressed a desire for negotiations with a view to enabling it to participate in the extension of E.E.C. in a form which would be compatible with a continued Swedish policy of neutrality', while, in an accompanying memorandum, the Swedish Government stated that it did 'not wish to exclude any of the forms laid down in the Treaty of Rome for participating in an enlarged E.E.C.' Meantime (11 July 1967) the E.E.C. Council had approved the text of 'a mandate for the Commission to open a first stage of negotiations with Spain, an issue that has long been under examination in the Community'.† At the same time the Council expressed a desire for the resumption of negotiations with Tunisia and Morocco (a progress report on which was submitted to the Council on 25 July). Several years earlier (1 November 1962) an Association Agreement between the European Economic Community and Greece had come into force; an Association Agreement had also been made with Turkey (1963) and Nigeria had

*September 1967.   †ibid.

signed an Association Agreement with the Community in July 1966.

Events, and decisions in specific instances, were thus outpacing decisions regarding fundamental principles. Yet, as early as 1959, the Foreign Ministers of the six Community countries had given the first practical expression to a resolve to extend the economic unity of Europe to the political level. In a communiqué issued at a meeting in Strasbourg on 23 November of that year they stated: 'The six Foreign Ministers have agreed to hold regular consultations on matters of international policy. These consultations will cover both the political implications of the activities of the European Communities and other international problems... the six Ministers will meet every three months.'

During 1960 the political organization of Europe was discussed at meetings between the President of the French Republic and the Prime Ministers and Foreign Ministers of the six Community countries. French ideas on the subject were first made public at a press conference given by the President of the Republic on 5 September, during which he stated:

The rebuilding of Europe – that is, its unification – is clearly essential. To say this is to utter a commonplace. Why should this great source of civilization, of strength, reason and prosperity be allowed to expire beneath its own ashes?

However, in a sphere such as this, one should not cling to dreams but be guided by realities.

Now, what are the realities, what are the pillars upon which Europe can be built?

These are, in fact, the States – States that while undoubtedly differing widely one from the other, each possessing a soul, a history and language of its own, its own misfortunes, glories and ambitions, are the sole entities endowed with the right to command and to be obeyed.

To imagine that something effective could be created and win the approval of the peoples without the assent of the States, is to indulge in fantasy.

It is true that, pending the time when the problem of Europe can be tackled as a whole, it has been possible to set up certain bodies of a more or less extra- or supra-national character. These bodies have their technical value but do not, and cannot, exert authority or effective political influence. So long as nothing serious occurs, they function without much trouble; but as soon as a dramatic issue is raised, as soon as a major problem has to be solved, it is immediately found that this or that high authority has no control over the various national groups. That such control lies exclusively in the hands of the States was demonstrated not long ago at the time of the coal crisis and was further borne out by the problems raised in the Common Market in respect of agricultural products, economic aid to certain African states and relations between the Common Market and the Free Trade Area.

It is again quite natural that the States of Europe should be able to call on specialized bodies to deal with their common problems, to prepare and, if need be, follow up their decisions. These decisions, however, must be taken by the States themselves. They alone can take such decisions, which can be reached only on the basis of cooperation.

France considers that regular cooperation between the States of Western Europe in the political, economic, cultural and defence fields is not only desirable but both possible and practical.

What precisely does this involve? It involves organized, regular and concerted action by the responsible Governments, and the contributions of bodies that specialize in each of the common fields and are subject to the control of the Governments.

It involves periodic meetings of an Assembly consisting of delegates from the national Parliaments. As I see it, it also calls for a solemn European referendum to be held as soon as possible so as to ensure for this European undertaking the popular support and participation which is essential to it.

It so happens that the States of Europe today possess, individually and in common, considerable resources; at the same time they are faced with considerable common problems.

Former enmities have been reduced to insignificant proportions. Briefly, an opportunity has now arrived to introduce cooperation between them. This is what France proposes.

If – as is to be hoped – this path is chosen, links will be forged and, in the course of time, it may be possible to take bigger strides towards European unity. This, once again, is what France proposes, this and nothing else.

Meetings between the Heads of State or Government and the Foreign Ministers of the six countries were held in February 1961 (Paris) and in July 1961 (Bonn). The communiqué issued on the conclusion of the latter meeting declared the Heads of State to be united in an awareness of the great tasks that Europe is called upon to fulfil within the community of free peoples in order to safeguard freedom and peace in the world; anxious to strengthen the political, economic, social, and cultural ties that exist between their peoples, especially in the framework of the European Communities, and to advance towards the union of Europe;

convinced that only a united Europe, allied to the United States of America and to other free peoples, is in a position to face the dangers that menace the existence of Europe and of the whole free world, and that it is important to pool the energies, capabilities, and resources of all for whom liberty is an inalienable possession; resolved to develop their political cooperation with a view to the union of Europe and to continue at the same time the work already undertaken in the European Communities;

desiring the adhesion to the European Communities of other European States ready to assume in all spheres the same responsibilities and the same obligations, have decided

(1) To give shape to the will for political union already implicit in the treaties establishing the European Communities, and for the purpose to organize their cooperation to provide for its development and to secure for it the regularity which will progressively create the conditions for a common policy and will ultimately make it possible to embody in institutions the work undertaken;

(2) To hold, at regular intervals, meetings whose aim will be to compare their views, to concert their policies and to reach common positions in order to further the political union of Europe, thereby strengthening the Atlantic Alliance. The necessary practical measures will be taken to prepare these meetings. In addition, the continuation of active cooperation among the Foreign Ministers will contribute to the continuity of the action undertaken in common. The cooperation of the Six must go beyond the political field as such, and will in particular be extended to the sphere of education, of culture, and of research, where it will be ensured by periodical meetings of the Ministers concerned;

(3) To instruct the Committee to submit to them proposals on the means by which a statutory form can be given as soon as possible to the union of their peoples.

The Heads of State or Government are convinced that by thus organizing their cooperation, they will further the application of the Treaties of Paris and Rome. They also believe that their cooperation will facilitate any reforms that might appear opportune in the interests of the Communities' greater efficiency.

To this end they have decided:

(1) To have a study made of the various points of the resolution of the European Parliament of 29 June 1961 on political cooperation among the member States of the European Communities;

(2) To associate public opinion more closely with the efforts already undertaken, by inviting the European Parliament to extend to new fields, with the cooperation of the Governments, the range of its debates.

The steps taken consequent upon this communiqué can be briefly summarized as follows. The Committee instructed by the Bonn Conference to study the Statute of the Political Union, appointed the French representative, M. Fouchet, as its chairman. A first draft treaty was submitted by him to the Committee on 2 November 1961. On 21 December the European Parliament adopted a number of recommendations in respect of the draft. A second draft was submitted to the Fouchet Committee on 18 January 1962 by the French representative, but it was apparently not accepted as a basis for discussion by the other five delegations. It appeared to have disregarded their suggestions and, indeed, to be a step backwards from the first drafts. Following this meeting the other five delegations in turn prepared a draft of the treaty. The Fouchet Committee met again on 20 February, but the two French drafts were not improved upon to general satisfaction, the main subject of disagreement being the danger that the contemplated Council of Heads of State or Government might gradually undermine the existing Communities. At a further meeting on 15 March 1962 disagreement persisted and appeared to centre on the inclusion of economic affairs among the tasks of the Union, as well as upon the relationship of the Union to the Atlantic Alliance and the provisions to be included in the treaty of Union for its own subsequent review. As a compromise, the Fouchet Committee adopted a fourth draft treaty containing a joint text of those articles on which all six delegations were agreed, and alternative texts of those articles as to which they were not agreed, showing the proposals of the French delegation on the one hand and the proposals of the other five delegations on the other hand. At a meeting of the Foreign Ministers on 20 March, disagreement persisted concerning both the overall concept of the Union and the provisions for treaty review: a fresh mandate was given to the Committee, due to meet again on 5 April, and the Head of the Italian delegation (Mr Cattani) was appointed chairman in the place of M. Fouchet who had been assigned other duties by his government. On 10 April 1962, Mr Heath, Lord Privy Seal, speaking in London at a meeting of the Council of Ministers of Western European Union,* officially requested that the United Kingdom be invited to take part in the negotiations for European political union. The Foreign Ministers of the Six met again in Paris on 17 April, but in spite of an attempt at reconciliation on the basis of a re-wording of the draft in respect of the Atlantic Alliance and the preservation of the existing Communities, disagreement over the review clause and the participation of the United Kingdom persisted. On 15 May the President of the French Republic gave a press conference giving his answers to two questions regarding the political union: the reasons which led France to submit a plan for the political organization of the Six, and his own views regarding the objections to that plan made both abroad and in France (especially during a recent debate in the National Assembly). The Italian Government and Mr Cattani continued their efforts to bring about a reconciliation, as a last resort through diplomatic channels; but these were not successful. Franco–German negotiations for a bi-lateral treaty commenced in September, so it appeared pointless to hold a 'summit' meeting of the Six. On 22 January 1963 the Franco–German Treaty was signed in Paris. There the matter rested.

Though no tangible progress has been made towards political union of the Six there are several lessons to be derived from the negotiations that are directly related to the theme of this book.

The first French draft (No. 1961) contained, as the heading of its 'Title I', the name 'Union of the European Peoples'. Those words were followed immediately by

Article 1. By the present Treaty, a Union of States, hereafter called 'the Union', is established. The Union is based on respect for the individuality of the peoples and of the Member States and for equality of rights and obligations. It is indissoluble.

*See Chapter 2.

A month later (December 1961) the European Parliament passed a series of recommendations concerning the draft, and, in respect of Article 1, noted

that the term 'Union of States' used in the draft does not correspond either with the ideas or with the wording of the declaration published on 18th July after the Bonn meeting. The communiqué envisaged a union of the European peoples. The contents of the new treaty should tally with that document.

After its meeting in March 1962 the drafting committee issued an explanatory report, which, in respect of Article 1, had this to say:

The French delegation does not consider it desirable at the present stage to describe the Union as a union of European peoples. It feels that, regardless of the terminology used in the Bonn declaration of 18 July 1961, the contemplated Union cannot yet be regarded as associating the European peoples. In order not to depreciate the term or the idea it expresses, the French delegation thinks it would be best to refrain from using it until later, as and when the Union makes sufficient progress. The other delegates feel that such progress should be provided for in the treaty. They therefore feel they can already make use of the term 'Union of Peoples' inasmuch as the article providing for a general review guarantees the progressive association of the peoples with the activities of the Union, particularly through the direct election of the European Parliament.

What's in a name? In this instance, certainly, a very great deal was in the name. For, basically, there was a clear division between the French school of thought and the rest. The latter considered that political union would be positively achieved by a continuance and extension of the 'community method' and therefore should be legally and constitutionally established from the beginning on comparable lines. The existing European Communities, transcending the frontiers of nation States, had brought individuals and associations of individuals, as well as the States to which they belonged, into a new form of human grouping: the treaty for political union should do likewise. Political union was, after all, what the existing Communities were intended to grow into. The French, on the other hand, took the view that the only effective agencies for the operation of political union in practical terms were the States themselves. This view had indeed been publicly expressed by the President of the French Republic at the press conference on 5 September 1960, to which reference has already been made.*

Yet there was never any divergence of opinion between the view of the French and of the rest that the treaty should bring into being a legal person (and the wording of the relevant article was made identical with that of Article 210 of the E.E.C. Treaty, and equivalent articles in the two other community treaties). Had the treaty merely envisaged cooperation of States, and not integration, no such provision would have been necessary – as the discussion of the differences between E.F.T.A. and the Communities at the beginning of this chapter attempted to show.

Consonant with the Union being a legal person was the provision in both drafts (that is, the French and the draft of the other five) for it to have Institutions. But the drafts differed in the following way: The French wanted a Council, Committees of Ministers, a Political Commission, and the European Parliament to be the Union's Institutions. The other five wanted the Council, the Committees of Ministers, and the European Parliament, and to make it clear that the Political Commission was not to resemble the Commissions of the existing Communities, but to function as an advisory body to assist the Council and the Committee of Ministers. Since the Commission envisaged for the Union was to be inter-governmental, the Dutch delegation preferred to avoid calling it by a name which would not distinguish it from the Community Commission. The other five, unlike the French, wanted the Court of Justice of the existing Communities to act as an Institution of the new Union.

In its explanatory report the Committee pointed out that it was

extremely difficult to arrive at a satisfactory definition of the composition of the Council that takes account not only of the desire of most of the delegations that the Council should meet at the highest level but also of the constitutional requirements and the customs in force in each State. A definition must be found that simultaneously covers the case of meetings attended only by Heads of State, or by Heads of State and their Prime Ministers, meetings attended only by Prime Ministers or

*See the extracts from the press conference pp. 152–3.

by Foreign Ministers, and meetings attended by Prime Ministers and their Foreign Ministers. A further difficulty lies in the fact that the term 'Head of the Executive' has different connotations in certain member States.

The simplest formula, according to the Belgian delegation, would be that of the Treaty of Rome; some delegations, however, fear that its application might detract from the high-level status it is desired to confer on the Council.

There were divergencies of view on certain aspects of the Council's functioning: its presidency, participation in its deliberations by the institutions of the existing Communities, and the unanimity rule. The Committee report explained:

Several delegations feel that the sequence of rotation and the term of office of the President should correspond with those of the E.E.C.

The Italian and German delegations, however, believe that a longer term of office would promote continuity in the work of the Council.

The German delegation desired that express provision should be made for inviting the Commissions and the High Authority of the existing Communities to take part in Council meetings in so far as matters falling within their competence were involved.

A provision of this nature appeared dangerous as it was liable to be read as a contradiction of the highly important principle that the competence of the Union and of the existing Communities should be kept separate. In theory, respect for this principle precludes the possibility of the same problems being discussed in the Union and in the Communities, at all events during the first stage of the Union.

Should a question arise that does not fall clearly within the province of either the Union or the Communities, it would have to be settled through consultation between the Council and the Communities.

For its part, the French delegation considers that, if it is neither desirable nor possible to limit the competence of the Heads of State or Government, it is likewise unnecessary to lay down the procedure the Council should follow from case to case.

The delegations tried to find a way of avoiding the difficulties created by strict observance of the unanimity rule. Apart from the solutions outlined in Article 7, certain delegations envisaged the following possible exceptions to this rule:

(1) An exception applying particularly to questions connected with joint intervention by member States of the Union within certain international organizations. A qualified majority, with the same

apportionment of votes as that laid down in the Treaties of Rome, would be fixed for this purpose.

(2) As soon as the Union came into force, the Council would rule by an absolute majority of member States on procedural questions and on whether a matter was one of procedure or substance.

(3) The Council would rule by a simple majority on matters relating to the rules of procedure or to financial and administrative regulations.

The French delegation regards the unanimity rules as essential. Nevertheless, the text proposed by it includes a clause whereby the Council could, with the unanimous agreement of the member States, take decisions that were binding on only four or five of these States.

As to the binding effect on member States of decisions taken by the Council the divergencies of view showed up clearly in the drafts. The French draft provided (Article 7):

The decisions of the Council shall be implemented by member States that have participated in their adoption. Member States that are not bound by a decision, by reason of their absence or abstention, may endorse it at any time. From the moment they endorse it, the decision shall be binding on them.

The draft of the other five read:

The decisions of the Council shall be carried out in accordance with the constitutional requirements in force in each member State. The Council may, by a unanimous decision, waive the principle of unanimity in specific cases. The abstention of one or two members shall not prevent decisions requiring unanimity from being taken.

As to the Court of Justice, it is not clear from the committee report which were the 'certain delegations' who considered that member States should be permitted to confer on the Court 'general competence to settle any disputes that may arise'. (One of the recommendations made by the European Parliament, after its examination of the first French draft, was a proposal 'to the Governments that the jurisdiction of the Court of Justice of the European Communities should be extended to the new organization in so far as the interpretation of the treaty or of its implementing provisions is concerned'.)

The objectives of the Union – a most important matter – could not be generally agreed upon in the Committee. The French draft (Article 2) had stated: 'It shall be the aim of the Union to reconcile, coordinate and unify the policy of member States in spheres of common interest: foreign policy, economics, cultural affairs and defence'. The draft of the other five was far more specific (hence longer) and also provided protection as against the Union, for the existing and growing role of the European Communities:

1. It shall be the task of the European Union to promote the unity of Europe by reconciling, coordinating and unifying the policy of member States.

2. For the purpose of accomplishing this task, the objectives of the Union shall be: the adoption of a common foreign policy; the adoption of a common defence policy [within the framework of the Atlantic Alliance]; [as a contribution towards strengthening the Atlantic Alliance] close cooperation in the educational, scientific and cultural fields; the harmonization and unification of the laws of member States; the settlement, in a spirit of mutual understanding and constructive cooperation of any differences that may arise in relations between member States.

3. Objectives other than those laid down in the preceding paragraph may be defined by the Council after consultation with the European Parliament.

4. This treaty shall not derogate from the competence of the European Communities.

By way of explanation, the Committee report had this to say:

The French delegation feels that in view of the fact that the Council, as supreme organ of the Union, is composed of persons who bear the highest degree of responsibility in their respective countries, it must be able to deal with all problems affecting their countries' interests in any sphere. The French delegation maintains that the value of such a comparison of viewpoints is indisputable.

Article 2 of the 'five other delegations' is the result of a compromise between two slightly different ways of envisaging the competence of the Union.

In the view of four delegations (those of Belgium, Germany, Italy and Luxemburg), the Union's competence should complement that of the existing Communities and should be of a residuary nature so as to enable the Union to supplement the Communities in all aspects of the policy of member States. It is in this spirit that paragraph 1 uses the word 'policy' without limiting it by the qualification 'of common interest'. These four delegations would have preferred the objectives of the Union to have been enumerated by reference to examples.

The Dutch delegation, on the other hand, feels that the enumeration of objectives should be restrictive in order to establish beyond doubt that member States retain any powers that have not been specifically conferred on the Union.

A compromise between these two tendencies was reached by retaining the words 'the policy' in paragraph 1 and a restrictive enumeration of the present objectives of the Union in paragraph 2, and by introducing a relatively simple procedure in paragraph 3 so as to allow the scope of the Union's objectives to be extended.

The 'five other delegations' consider that it should be expressly stipulated that the competence and objectives of the Union must not encroach on those of the existing European Communities. They propose that paragraph 4 should be interpreted as excluding from the sphere of activity of the Union not only the existing powers of the Communities but also the initiative allowed them under Article 235 of the treaty establishing the E.E.C., Article 203 of the treaty establishing the E.A.E.C. and Article 95 of the treaty establishing the E.C.S.C. It should be noted that paragraph 4 does not rule out the possibility of the constitution of the European Union envisaged in Article 20 (2) incorporating the Union and the Communities in an organic institutional framework.

The 'five other delegations' consider that it should be expressly stipulated that the Union must not interfere with the competence of NATO but, on the contrary, as in any case laid down in the Bonn Declaration of 18 July, must strengthen that alliance. The Dutch delegation wishes to make it quite clear that the common defence policy laid down in Article 2 as an objective of the Union must remain 'within the framework of the Atlantic Alliance' so as to provide an objective criterion for Union policy in the field of defence.

With regard to the unification of laws as an objective of the Union, it was agreed that at a later stage, and in the light of the progress achieved by the Union, provision could be made for the Council to specify the spheres in which it felt that harmonization or unification of laws was desirable.

For this purpose, the Council, after consulting with the European Parliament, would issue directives under the terms of Article 7.

The German delegation regarded the concept of European Citizenship, which it would have liked to be introduced into the Treaty, as a necessary corollary to the unification of laws. It also felt it desirable to express in this way, through outward symbols, the common membership of the States and peoples in the Union – regarding which factor disagreement had been clearly manifest, as mentioned earlier, in the discussions on Article 1.

For much of the Preamble to the draft treaty the French delegation and the other five were able to reach agreement on a joint text. What are most revealing of the trends of thought in the early 1960s – trends that are probably little changed at the time of writing – are the nuances of difference both in those parts of the Preamble on which they could not agree, and in the successive amendments to the first French draft which enabled much agreement to be reached.

All six delegations eventually agreed the following opening paragraph of the Preamble:

THE HIGH CONTRACTING PARTIES

Convinced that the union of Europe in freedom and respect for its diversity will permit its civilization to develop, add to the prestige of its spiritual heritage, increase its capacity to defend itself against external threats, facilitate the contribution it makes to the progress of other peoples and contribute [in keeping with the principles of the United Nations Charter] to world peace;

In this paragraph, 'the organization of Europe' (first and second French draft) became 'the union of Europe'; 'in freedom and respect its diversity' had been 'in a spirit of freedom and of respect for its diversity' (second French draft) and previously 'in a spirit of freedom that respects its diversity' (first French draft); the words from 'add to ... threats' were identical with the second French draft, but the first French draft had read 'protect their common spiritual heritage from any threats to which it may be exposed'; the words, in the joint text, from 'following' to 'world peace', were (except for the reference in brackets to the U.N. Charter regarding which the delegations could not agree) identical with the second French draft – the first French draft having read:

163

'and in this way contribute to the maintenance of peaceful relations in the world'.

The second paragraph of the Preamble was agreed by all six delegations as follows:

Affirming their attachment to the principles of democracy, to respect for law and to social justice;

The first and second French drafts had included the first phrase of the paragraph (as far as 'the principles of democracy') in identical terms. But the first French draft had continued (thereby evoking the Declaration of 1793 and successive French constitutions) with 'to the rights of man and to justice in every sphere of social life'. In the second French draft 'the rights of man' became 'Human Rights', and was evocative of the European Convention on that subject. The effect virtually would have been to impose recognition of European standards in this matter, as expressed in the Convention, on any European state wishing to adhere to the political union.

The third paragraph of the joint text agreed by all six delegations was identical with the second French draft, and with the first part of the first French draft (which added 'and to work for the advent of a better world in which these values would permanently prevail'). The joint text read:

Resolved jointly to safeguard the dignity, freedom and equality of men, regardless of their status, race or creed;

When it came to expressing in the Preamble the general relationship of the work of the European Communities to political union a joint text could not be agreed upon. The Committee was therefore left with the second French draft, reading:

Resolved to pursue the task of reconciling their essential interests already initiated, in their respective fields, by the European Coal and Steel Community, the European Economic Community and the European Atomic Energy Community;

and with the draft of the other five delegations, containing a very significant addition at the end, as well as a meaningful change at the outset:

Resolved to pursue the task of reconciling their essential interests, already the objective, in their respective fields, of the European Coal and Steel Community, the European Economic Community and the European Atomic Energy Community, in order to lay the foundation for a destiny to be irrevocably shared;

The Preamble continued with a joint text from which all disagreements between the six delegations (in respect of the words in brackets) could not be eliminated:

[Desirous of welcoming] [Ready to welcome] to their ranks other countries of Europe that are prepared to accept in every sphere the same responsibilities and the same obligations [and conscious of thus forming the nucleus of a union, membership of which will be open to other peoples of Europe that are as yet unable to take such a decision];

There was general agreement with the concluding premise of the Preamble:

Resolved to this end, to give statutory form to the union of their peoples, in accordance with the declaration of 18 July 1961 by the Heads of State or Government:

HAVE APPOINTED AS THEIR PLENIPOTENTIARIES: ...

6

Other Potential Members

As the last chapter showed, there has since 1962 been a pause in the formulation of a treaty for the union of the European peoples. But in the meantime the conviction – amongst the majority of European Governments (including the British) as well as amongst the peoples of Europe – that it is into such a union that the existing Communities must blossom out, has almost certainly not weakened. Perhaps it has even strengthened. Certainly there have been voices raised to re-affirm the notion expressed by the five in the draft Preamble to the 1962 formulation, that the pursuit of the task of reconciling the essential interests of member States and their peoples, begun by the European Communities, was 'in order to lay the foundation for a destiny to be irrevocably shared'. These words, as was to be expected, were taken up – as has been mentioned earlier – by the Commission of E.E.C. in its Annual Report for 1967, and the same notion has been variously expressed by many others.

While there has been a pause on the political front between the member States, the Communities themselves have been far from inactive in the field of their international economic relationships. Around the nucleus of the Six, there have already been gathered, in economic association, Greece, Turkey and Nigeria, while other countries may soon follow this example; a number of countries, as is well known, seek not association with the Communities but direct membership.

In this chapter, it is proposed to consider briefly, from a legal point of view, some of the countries in both these categories which are European, in order to note in what ways they may exemplify particular aspects or problems of wider European unification in the next few years.

GREECE

The first two Association Agreements made by the European Economic Community were with Greece (1962) and Turkey (1963). Both are directed to the establishment by stages of a complete customs union between the Community and the Associates. There is no commitment by either the Community or the Associates that the latter will, at some time following the establishment of a complete customs union, become members of the Community. But this, at least in the case of Greece, has been declared to be the objective, and it would seem that in practice little would stand in the way of their membership once full customs union was reached, because the very fact of reaching it would go a long way to demonstrating that, economically, the Associates were now strong and resilient enough to become full members. Unless, that is, there is to be also some political test of their fitness to join.

In the uncertainty that at the moment exists regarding the blossoming of the Community into a political union, and regarding the questions of general policy facing the Community before that comes about* (these questions being inevitably in some degree political and not exclusively economic), this is obviously not a matter that can be examined by the Community as such on the basis of existing agreed principles. So, when the revolution in Greece in 1967 led to installation of an undemocratic régime and the revocation of Article 18 of the Greek Constitution ('Torture and general confiscation are prohibited. Civil death is abolished. The penalty of death for purely political offences is abolished'),† there was an inevitable effect on that country's association with the Community. In particular, the programme of financial assistance by the Community, to enable the Greek economy to develop more rapidly, was allowed to grind to a halt.

This result is not traceable to a positive decision of the Community as such. In the first place, the question of whether or not the new government should be accorded legal recognition, as a

* See Chapter 5.

† Restored in vertually identical wording in the final draft of the new Constitution as Article 11 (3), except for compound political crimes.

matter of international law, was not a question properly pertaining to the Community itself, but to its member States severally and individually. This situation represented, in fact, one further example of the incompleteness of the international legal personality of the Community, which has been briefly discussed in the preceding chapter. The Treaty of Association had been entered into by Greece, on the one hand, and seven entities on the other – namely, each of the six member States and the Community itself. In the event, therefore, each member State took such diplomatic action with regard to the new Greek regime as it deemed necessary and according to its accustomed practices. But the attitudes of the individual member States could not fail to find some echo in the Council of Association which had been set up by the treaty to 'ensure the application and progressive development of the régime of association' between the contracting parties (Article 3).

Irrespective of the fact that eight entities, in all, joined in the making of the treaty, the Association is recognized to rest in essence on a bilateral agreement between Greece, constituting one party, and the seven entities constituting collectively the other party. A glance at the nature of the Council of Association bears out the bilateral essence of the agreement. For example, Article 65 (1) reads:

For the attainment of the objects of the present agreement, and in the cases provided for in it, the Council of Association shall dispose of a power of decision. Each of the *two* Parties is under an obligation to take the measures necessary for the execution of the decisions taken. ... (present author's italics).

This aspect is enlarged upon in Article 65 (3):

The Council of Association is composed, on the one hand, of members of the Governments of the member States, of the Council and of the Commission of the Community and, on the other hand, of members of the Greek Government. ...

Article 65 (4) concludes the treaty provisions for the organization and functioning of the Council of Association with the words: 'The Council of Association decides by unanimous vote.'

Thus, there could hardly be surprise when on 28 November 1967, the President of the Council of Association informed the European Parliament that further development of the Association had been suspended. The agreement was still in force because it had been concluded with the Greek State and not with the government; but the development of the Association had now been blocked, he said, with particular regard to harmonization of agricultural policies and the negotiation of a new financial protocol. The President of the Council further pointed out that the agreement with Greece was not exclusively economic, in that its ultimate objective was Greek membership of the Community. (A glance at the headings of the sections into which the treaty is divided makes this fact abundantly clear. By a phased progression there is to be, within the Association, 'Free Movement of Goods' based on a Customs Union and adoption by Greece of the common external tariff, on elimination of quantitative restrictions between the contracting parties, and on agriculture and 'Free Movement of Persons and Services'. There are also 'Provisions regarding Competition, Taxation, and the Harmonization of Laws'.)

The text of a new Constitution for Greece was adopted after a referendum on 29 September 1968.* Government and people now have the task of effecting a smooth transition from the regulatory requirements of the military régime to a full implementation of the new Constitution, in itself a thoroughly democratic conception.

'The form of Government in Greece is that of a Crowned Democracy. All powers emanate from the People, exist in favour of the People and the Nation, and are exercised in the manner provided by the Constitution,' stated Article 2 of the final draft. Article 3 laid down a clear separation of powers: 'The judicial power is exercised by the courts. Judicial decisions are executed in the name of the King' whilst 'the legislative power is exercised by the King and Parliament' and 'the executive power is exercised by the King and the Government.' But note that 'with the exception of the Prime Minister and Deputy Prime Ministers no member of Parliament may be appointed member of the Govern-

* pp. 169–71 were brought up to date at a late stage. [E.W.]

ment, even though he may resign his parliamentary office'
(Article 88 (2)) and that 'a member of the Government, with
the exception of the Prime Minister (and Deputy), may not submit candidature for the immediately forthcoming elections even
though he had resigned before the termination of the parliamentary session' (Article 61 (5)). These factors may contribute to a
speeding up of the legislative process – formerly often dilatory. It
may also be noted that 'on special occasions of extraordinarily
urgent and unforeseeable necessity the King shall have the right,
on recommendation of the Council of Ministers, and with the
concurring opinion of the Constitutional Court as to urgency, to
issue legislative decrees' – which lapse if not approved by Parliament within three months (Article 48 (4)).

The Constitutional Court is a new feature in Greece. Its wide
powers (Article 106 (1–4)) range from rulings on 'the construction and extent of the powers of the principal state organs' to
decisions on 'appeals against legislative or administrative acts', on
electoral law, on 'the constitutionality of a law or legislative
decree, or specific provisions thereof' (when conflicting decisions
as to these have been arrived at by the Council of State, the
Supreme Court, or the Council of Comptrollers) 'upon petition
by the Minister of Justice or anyone having a lawful interest' – as
well as in every other case submitted to its jurisdiction by the
Constitution. Among the latter may figure the deprivation of
civil rights of 'who ever abuses the inviolability of a home, the
freedom of expression, especially in print, the secrecy of the
means of correspondence, the freedom of assembly, the freedom
to form associations or cooperatives, and the right of property, for
the purpose of combatting the political system of Crowned
Democracy, civil liberties, or of endangering national independence, and territorial integrity of the country' (Article 24).
(Unions of persons having similar objectives to the above or
directed against the principles of the régime or the social order
are prohibited and dissolved by court decree. 'The charter of
every political party must be approved by the Constitutional
Court' – Article 58 (2) .)

Since one function of the Constitutional Court is to pronounce
upon the constitutionality of laws [and legislative decrees], it

would appear that enactments resulting from eventual Greek membership of the European Community may in principle be within its purview. This might conceivably extend to a statutory re-enactment of the Community Treaty itself because, although 'the King shall represent the Nation internationally and ... shall conclude international treaties or conventions except those concluded by other officials upon whom the necessary authority has been conferred by law', 'treaties, or trade and other agreements which according to the provisions of the Constitution require a law, or which impose burdens on Greeks individually, shall have no force without statutory law enactment' (Article 53 (1), (3)).

If Greece eventually becomes a Community member, she would bring with her a Western European system of ordinary law and a considerable experience of administrative law, currently administered as a distinct body of law, both by the ordinary courts and also by special administrative courts headed by the Council of State.

TURKEY

The case of Turkey, from the point of view of ultimate membership of the Community, would appear on present showing to be essentially one of economics – not one of politics and economics combined, as is that of Greece. If Turkey is to become a member, probably the essential question is how soon her economy, which is primarily agricultural, can be strong enough to take the strains of full membership. As far as the constitutional law and general law of Turkey is concerned, it seems that nothing would stand in the way of her membership or obstruct its efficient operation.

The ordinary law of Turkey now contains a large amount of law from Western European sources, and incorporated directly and intentionally into the national system. Thus the Code of Obligations of 1926 which regulates contracts, the Commercial Code, the Civil Code and the Code of Civil Procedure all show such influences or origins. The judges are independent of the other arms of government and exercise jurisdiction in civil, commercial and criminal cases. There are no juries, and no courts of appeal as to questions of fact – though the Supreme Court ('cassation' on the French model) may be appealed to on points of law. The judgments of the Supreme Court are held to be final, though in certain special circumstances the court is entitled to reconsider a judgment already delivered. Turkey does not have a special administrative jurisdiction. There is, however, a Constitutional Court to watch over a very modern Constitution adopted on 9 July 1961.

In the Constitution, the Turkish State is defined (Article 1) as a republic based on the principles of human rights, and as a national, democratic, secular and social (i.e. welfare) State bound by the rule of law (Article 2). Sovereignty is unconditionally vested in the nation, and no exclusive person, group or class, can under any circumstances be entrusted with the exercise of sovereign power.

A series of some fifty articles of the Constitution (10–62) provide specifically for virtually all democratic and civil liberties, rights and obligations. Thus, for example, personal liberty and domicile are expressed to be inviolable except where provided by law and authorized by the Judiciary (Article 14). Freedom of speech and writing (Article 20), press (Article 22), movement (Article 18), meeting (Article 28) and association (Article 29) are also safeguarded.

Amongst the social and economic rights vouchsafed by the constitution figure the following: The right of private property is recognized, and can be limited only by law. Its use may not be contrary to the public interest (Article 36) and expropriation of private property in the public interest is possible only if the real value of the property is paid (Article 38). Proper working conditions for employees (Article 43) and holidays with pay (Article 44) are requisite, while the organization of trade unions is free (Article 46) and the rights of collective bargaining and of strike action are recognized (Article 47).

As to the political rights of Turkish citizens, the Law on Elections of 1921 grants the vote to every individual at the age of twenty-one. The ballot is personal, equal, free, secret and direct.

Political parties can be founded without prior approval (Article 56 of the Constitution) but they are bound to adhere to the principles of human rights and of a law republic (Article 57). 'The Turkish Grand National Assembly', or Parliament, is made up of two 'Houses' – the National Assembly consisting of 450 representatives elected by direct suffrage, and the Senate of the Republic made up of sixteen members appointed by the President of the Republic and a further 150 members chosen by direct universal ballot.

NORWAY

Amongst the countries that have applied for membership it does not seem that the legal system of any one of them creates any unusual difficulties – unless the specific provision of Article 97 of the Constitution of Norway is regarded as likely to do so. 'No law may be given retroactive effect', it states. Of course, many legal systems lean firmly against retroactive legislation, the British system included. Yet, in the British system, the retroactive effect of fiscal legislation, for example, may appear on occasion unavoidable, however undesirable. In the Communities the retroactive effect of rule-making may sometimes be a requisite. Apart from that particular item, which might not turn out to be an insuperable obstacle, neither the Constitution nor the general law of Norway would seem to present any particular impediment to her working membership of the Communities. It is of interest, however, recalling the outline given at the beginning of this book of the evolution of government in the western states, to record that Norway is a 'hereditary democratic kingdom' with a constitution based on the strict separation of powers as conceived by Montesquieu, promulgated on the 17 May 1814 and still virtually unchanged – except for the important innovation of 1884 whereby Ministers were made dependent on 'Parliament'.

SWEDEN

Sweden, in applying in 1967 for negotiations for Community membership – 'with a view to enabling Sweden to participate in the extension of the E.E.C. in a form which would be compatible with a continued Swedish policy of neutrality' without 'wishing to exclude any of the forms laid down in the Treaty of Rome for participating in an enlarged E.E.C.' – may have presented the Communities with a policy problem which for several years they have known they were most likely at some time to have to face. But it can hardly have presented any unusual economic or legal problem.

For the record, again, and recalling the opening part of this book, it is of interest, particularly to the British reader, that Sweden is also a country which has no single constitutional law. The Fundamental Statutes of Sweden are four in number: the Instrument of Government (1809), the Act of Succession (1810), the Parliament Act (1866) and the Freedom of the Press Act (1949). Parliamentary government is not embodied in the constitution but has been practised as a matter of constitutional custom since about 1900.

The legislative power in Sweden is shared between the King and the 'Parliament' (Riksdagen) – which has an upper and a lower House with equal competence and authority. The judicial power is independent of all other authority.

The Executive Power is vested by the Instrument of Government in the King as the personal and independent ruler, but in practice it has been transferred to the Council of State, which consists of the Ministers. The King is, however, personally present at the weekly meetings of this body, whose decisions are thus taken by the 'King in Council'. It is the King in Council which makes, for example, statutory instruments by way of implementation of statutes. Regulations may also be made within the limits of the Royal Prerogative. Such regulations and statutes as relate to special fields of administration or to special governmental agencies are looked upon as forming part of a body of law (administrative law) quite distinct from the law which governs the relations between citizens. The Swedish concept of administrative law resembles in this way that of France. But the concepts of administrative and public law in Sweden are not, as in France, the consequence of constitutional provisions or principles. They are the result of doctrinal development. It cannot therefore be said in Sweden, as it can in France,

that because a rule belongs to administrative law or public law it must be applied by administrative authorities and not by the ordinary courts. In every situation one must investigate whether the power to decide has been conferred on an administrative authority. If this is not the case the question belongs to the ordinary courts, even if it is regarded by doctrine as a matter of administrative law.*

When power to decide is given to an administrative authority, the corollary is a right of administrative appeal, which means that a case against the administration may be decided in the last resort by the 'King in Council', or, in other cases, by an administrative court. These principles are clearly by no means remote from those incorporated in the law of the European Communities. It may also perhaps be reasonably conjectured that subsidiary legislation by the Executive (the King in Council) in implementation of community law might be faced in Sweden with less reserve or hesitancy than it has in some present member States. In short, it would seem that the only question concerning Swedish membership of the Communities that might require a solution until now unprecedented is that of regard for her policy of neutrality. (The question of Austrian neutrality is, as pointed out earlier, somewhat different from that of Sweden, in the context of community membership.)

SPAIN

Spain submitted an application to the Communities for association and eventual membership, in February 1962. The political history of Spain in the last thirty years provoked a certain amount of

*Nils Herlitz, 'Swedish Administrative Law', *International and Comparative Law Quarterly*, April 1953, p. 225.

alarm in some quarters, amongst the member States, on the news of this application. It remained for a long time under examination in the E.E.C. On 11 July 1967 the E.E.C. Council approved the text of what 'European Community' described as 'a mandate for the E.E.C. Commission to open a first stage of negotiations for an agreement'* with Spain, and, at the time of writing a year later, information of progress is awaited.

A brief analysis of the constitutional and general legal systems that pertain in Spain does not throw up any obviously insoluble problems impeding either her association with or membership of the Communities. As declared by the Law of Succession approved by the Parliament (Cortes) on 16 July 1947, and confirmed by national referendum, Spain is a catholic, social and representative State, constituted as a Kingdom, in accordance with its tradition. The other fundamental laws are the Charter of the Spanish People (16 July 1945); the Act creating (or re-enacting) the Cortes of 17 July 1942, amended 9 March 1946; the Referendum Act of 22 October 1945; the Labour Charter of 6 July 1947. The source of sovereign power is not expressly defined in any of the fundamental laws, but is authoritatively considered to lie with the Spanish people.

The powers of the office of Chief of State (at present General Franco) will, in the event of a vacancy and in accordance with the Law of Succession, be assumed by a Council of Regency made up of the President of the Cortes, the highest ranking Prelate of the Catholic Church, and the highest ranking Officer of the Land, Sea and Air Forces.

Executive power is exercised by a government presided over by the Chief of State as Prime Minister. The supreme power to promulgate legal orders of a general nature remains vested in the Chief of State – so states the preamble to the Act of 1942 (as amended) creating the Cortes, so that the legislative role of that body is one of cooperation with the Chief of State. All laws prepared and made by the Cortes require the sanction of the Chief of State in order to take effect, while in time of war or emergency decree-laws may be made by the government on subjects which are within the competence of the Cortes, though

*European Community, September 1967.

they must be communicated to the Cortes at its first meeting after they are made. Two further forms of law are decrees and orders. Decrees are legal prescriptions emanating from the government in Council of Ministers, and signed by the Chief of State and the Minister who proposes them. Orders are legal prescriptions emanating from the Ministers, and signed by the Minister who issues them. So there exists a hierarchy of laws in the following descending sequence: Fundamental Laws, Laws (or Decree Laws), Decrees, Orders – and any legal rule inconsistent with one contained in a legal provision higher up in the hierarchy can be contested.

The Cortes, all of whose members are called 'Procuradores', contains both *ex officio* and elected members. The *ex officio* members are: the Ministers of State; the national councillors; the presidents of the Council of State, the Supreme Court of Justice, and the Supreme Court of Military Justice; the mayors of the fifty provincial capitals and of Ceuta and Melilla; and the presidents of the universities, the Institute of Spain, the higher council for scientific research, and the institute of civil engineers. A number of members not to exceed fifty may be appointed by the Chief of State on the basis of their ecclesiastical, administrative, military, or other public rank or their outstanding service to Spain. The remaining members are elected as follows: one by each of the municipalities other than the provincial capitals, Ceuta and Melilla; one by each of the provincial deputations and inter-island communal councils of the Canary Islands; two by the members of each of the royal academies belonging to the Institute of Spain; two by the members of the higher council for scientific research; one by the president of the association of engineers; two by the bar association; two by the medical association; one each by the pharmacists' association, the veterinarians' association, the architects' association, the association of bachelors and doctors of arts and sciences, the public notaries' association, the national corporation of registrars, and the association of solicitors; three by each of the official chambers of commerce; and a number, not to exceed one third of the total number of members of the Cortes, by the national syndicates.

No provision is made in the fundamental laws regarding the Judiciary (except special judges for labour disputes, provided for in the Labour Charter). The Judiciary operates in independence of the other areas of government, in accordance with custom and certain special laws. There are some courts exercising jurisdiction only in matters of administrative law.

The European Convention on Human Rights

Signed in Rome on 4 November 1950

The Governments signatory hereto, being Members of the Council of Europe.

Considering the Universal Declaration of Human Rights proclaimed by the General Assembly of the United Nations on 10 December 1948;

Considering that this Declaration aims at securing the universal and effective recognition and observance of the Rights therein declared;

Considering that the aim of the Council of Europe is the achievement of greater unity between its Members and that one of the methods by which that aim is to be pursued is the maintenance and further realization of Human Rights and Fundamental Freedoms;

Reaffirming their profound belief in those Fundamental Freedoms which are the foundation of justice and peace in the world and are best maintained on the one hand by an effective political democracy and on the other by a common understanding and observance of the Human Rights upon which they depend;

Being resolved, as the Governments of European countries which are like-minded and have a common heritage of political traditions, ideals, freedom and the rule of law to take the first steps for the collective enforcement of certain of the Rights stated in the Universal Declaration;

Have agreed as follows:

Article 1. The High Contracting Parties shall secure to everyone within their jurisdiction the rights and freedoms defined in Section I of this Convention.

SECTION 1

Article 2. (1) Everyone's right to life shall be protected by law. No one shall be deprived of his life intentionally save in the execution of a sentence of a court following his conviction of a crime for which this penalty is provided by law.

(2) Deprivation of life shall not be regarded as inflicted in contravention of this Article when it results from the use of force which is no more than absolutely necessary:

(*a*) in defence of any person from unlawful violence;

(*b*) in order to effect a lawful arrest or to prevent the escape of a person lawfully detained;

(*c*) in action lawfully taken for the purpose of quelling a riot or insurrection.

Article 3. No one shall be subjected to torture or to inhuman or degrading treatment or punishment.

Article 4. (1) No one shall be held in slavery or servitude.

(2) No one shall be required to perform forced or compulsory labour.

(3) For the purpose of this article the term 'forced or compulsory labour' shall not include:

(*a*) any work required to be done in the ordinary course of detention imposed according to the provisions of Article 5 of this Convention or during conditional release from such detention;

(*b*) any service of a military character or in case of conscientious objectors in countries where they are recognized, service exacted instead of compulsory military service;

(*c*) any service exacted in case of an emergency or calamity threatening the life or well-being of the community;

(*d*) any work or service which forms part of normal civic obligations.

Article 5. (1) Everyone has the right to liberty and security of person.

No one shall be deprived of his liberty save in the following cases and in accordance with a procedure prescribed by law;

(*a*) the lawful detention of a person after conviction by a competent court;

(*b*) the lawful arrest or detention of a person for non-compliance with the lawful order of a court or in order to secure the fulfilment of any obligation prescribed by law;

(*c*) the lawful arrest or detention of a person effected for the purpose of bringing him before the competent legal authority on reasonable suspicion of having committed an offence or when it is reasonably considered necessary to prevent his committing an offence or fleeing after having done so;

(*d*) the detention of a minor by lawful order for the purpose of educational supervision or his lawful detention for the purpose of bringing him before the competent legal authority;

(*e*) the lawful detention of persons for the prevention of the spreading of infectious diseases, of persons of unsound mind, alcoholics or drug addicts or vagrants;

(*f*) the lawful arrest or detention of a person to prevent his effecting an unauthorized entry into the country or of a person against whom action is being taken with a view to deportation or extradition.

(2) Everyone who is arrested shall be informed promptly, in a language which he understands, of the reasons for his arrest and of any charge against him.

(3) Everyone arrested or detained in accordance with the provisions of paragraph 1 (c) of this Article shall be brought promptly before a judge or other officer authorized by law to exercise judicial power and shall be entitled to trial within a reasonable time or to release pending trial. Release may be conditioned by guarantees to appear for trial.

(4) Everyone who is deprived of his liberty by arrest or detention shall be entitled to take proceedings by which the lawfulness of his detention shall be decided speedily by a court and his release ordered if the detention is not lawful.

(5) Everyone who has been the victim of arrest or detention in contravention of the provisions of this Article shall have an enforceable right to compensation.

Article 6. (1) In the determination of his civil rights and obligations or of any criminal charge against him, everyone is entitled to a fair and public hearing within a reasonable time by an independent and impartial tribunal established by law. Judgment shall be pronounced publicly but the press and public may be excluded from all or part of the trial in the interest of morals, public order or national security in a democratic society, where the interests of juveniles or the protection of the private life of the parties so require, or to the extent strictly necessary in the opinion of the court in special circumstances where publicity would prejudice the interests of justice.

(2) Everyone charged with a criminal offence shall be presumed innocent until proved guilty according to law.

(3) Everyone charged with a criminal offence has the following minimum rights:

(*a*) to be informed promptly, in a language which he understands and in detail, of the nature and cause of the accusation against him;

(*b*) to have adequate time and facilities for the preparation of his defence;

(*c*) to defend himself in person or through legal assistance of his own choosing or, if he has not sufficient means to pay for legal assistance, to be given it free when the interests of justice so require;

(*d*) to examine or have examined witnesses against him and to obtain the attendance and examination of witnesses on his behalf under the same conditions as witnesses against him;

(*e*) to have the free assistance of an interpreter if he cannot understand or speak the language used in court.

Article 7. (1) No one shall be held guilty of any criminal offence on account of any act or omission which did not constitute a criminal offence under national or international law at the time when it was committed. Nor shall a heavier penalty be imposed than the one that was applicable at the time the criminal offence was committed.

(2) This Article shall not prejudice the trial and punishment of any person for any act or omission which, at the time when it was

committed, was criminal according to the general principles of law recognized by civilized nations.

Article 8. (1) Everyone has the right to respect for his private and family life, his home and his correspondence.

(2) There shall be no interference by a public authority with the exercise of this right except such as is in accordance with the law and is necessary in a democratic society in the interests of national security, public safety or the economic well-being of the country, for the prevention of disorder or crime, for the protection of health or morals, or for the protection of the rights and freedoms of others.

Article 9. (1) Everyone has the right to freedom of thought, conscience and religion; this right includes freedom to change his religion or belief, and freedom, either alone or in community with others and in public or private, to manifest his religion or belief, in worship, teaching, practice and observance.

(2) Freedom to manifest one's religion or beliefs shall be subject only to such limitations as are prescribed by law and are necessary in a democratic society in the interests of public safety, for the protection of public order, health or morals, or for the protection of the rights and freedoms of others.

Article 10. (1) Everyone has the right to freedom of expression. This right shall include freedom to hold opinions and to receive and impart information and ideas without interference by public authority and regardless of frontiers. This Article shall not prevent States from requiring the licensing of broadcasting, television or cinema enterprises.

(2) The exercise of these freedoms, since it carries with it duties and responsibilities, may be subject to such formalities, conditions, restrictions or penalties as are prescribed by law and are necessary in a democratic society, in the interests of national security, territorial integrity or public safety, for the prevention of disorder or crime, for the protection of health or morals, for the protection of the reputation or rights of others, for preventing the disclosure of information received in confidence, or for maintaining the authority and impartiality of the judiciary.

Article 11. (1) Everyone has the right to freedom of peaceful assembly and to freedom of association with others, including the right to form and to join trade unions for the protection of his interests.

(2) No restrictions shall be placed on the exercise of these rights other than such as are prescribed by law and are necessary in a democratic society in the interests of national security or public safety, for the prevention of disorder or crime, for the protection of health or morals or for the protection of the rights and freedoms of others. This Article shall not prevent the imposition of lawful restrictions on the exercise of these rights by members of the armed forces, of the police or of the administration of the State.

Article 12. Men and women of marriageable age have the right to marry and to found a family, according to the national laws governing the exercise of this right.

Article 13. Everyone whose rights and freedoms as set forth in this Convention are violated shall have an effective remedy before a national authority notwithstanding that the violation has been committed by persons acting in an official capacity.

Article 14. The enjoyment of the rights and freedoms set forth in this Convention shall be secured without discrimination on any ground such as sex, race, colour, language, religion, political or other opinion, national or social origin, association with a national minority, property, birth or other status.

Article 15. (1) In time of war or other public emergency threatening the life of the nation any High Contracting Party may take measures derogating from its obligations under this Convention to the extent strictly required by the exigencies of the situation, provided that such measures are not inconsistent with its other obligations under international law.

(2) No derogation from Article 2, except in respect of deaths resulting from lawful acts of war, or from Articles 3, 4 (paragraph 1) and 7 shall be made under this provision.

(3) Any High Contracting Party availing itself of this right of derogation shall keep the Secretary-General of the Council of Europe fully informed of the measures which it has taken and the reasons therefor. It shall also inform the Secretary-General of the Council of Europe when such measures have ceased to operate and the provisions of the Convention are again being fully executed.

Article 16. Nothing in Articles 10, 11, and 14 shall be regarded as preventing the High Contracting Parties from imposing restrictions on the political activity of aliens.

Article 17. Nothing in this Convention may be interpreted as implying for any State, group or person any right to engage in any activity or perform any act aimed at the destruction of any of the rights and freedoms set forth herein or at their limitation to a greater extent than is provided for in the Convention.

Article 18. The restrictions permitted under this Convention to the said rights and freedoms shall not be applied for any purpose other than those for which they have been prescribed.

SECTION II

Article 19. To ensure the observance of the engagements undertaken by the High Contracting Parties in the present Convention, there shall be set up:

(1) A European Commission of Human Rights hereinafter referred to as 'the Commission';

(2) A European Court of Human Rights, hereinafter referred to as 'the Court'.

SECTION III

Article 20. The Commission shall consist of a number of members equal to that of the High Contracting Parties. No two members of the Commission may be nationals of the same State.

Article 21. (1) The members of the Commission shall be elected by the Committee of Ministers by an absolute majority of votes, from a list of names drawn up by the Bureau of the Consultative Assembly; each group of the Representatives of the High Contracting Parties in the Consultative Assembly shall put forward three candidates, of whom two at least shall be its nationals.

(2) As far as applicable, the same procedure shall be followed to complete the Commission in the event of other States subsequently becoming Parties to this Convention, and in filling casual vacancies.

Article 22. (1) The members of the Commission shall be elected for a period of six years. They may be re-elected. However, of the members elected at the first election, the terms of seven members shall expire at the end of three years.

(2) The members whose terms are to expire at the end of the initial period of three years shall be chosen by lot by the Secretary-General of the Council of Europe immediately after the first election has been completed.

(3) A member of the Commission elected to replace a member whose term of office has not expired shall hold office for the remainder of his predecessor's term.

(4) The members of the Commission shall hold office until replaced. After having been replaced, they shall continue to deal with such cases as they already have under consideration.

Article 23. The members of the Commission shall sit on the Commission in their individual capacity.

Article 24. Any High Contracting Party may refer to the Commission through the Secretary-General of the Council of Europe, any alleged breach of the provisions of the Convention by another High Contracting Party.

Article 25. (1) The Commission may receive petitions addressed to the Secretary-General of the Council of Europe from any person, non-governmental organization or group of individuals claiming to be the victim of a violation by one of the High Contracting Parties of the rights set forth in this Convention, provided that the High Contracting Party against which the complaint has been lodged has declared that it recognizes the competence of the Commission to receive such petitions. Those of the High Contracting Parties who have made such a declaration undertake not to hinder in any way the effective exercise of this right.

(2) Such declarations may be made for a specific period.

(3) The declarations shall be deposited with the Secretary-General of the Council of Europe who shall transmit copies thereof to the High Contracting Parties and publish them.

(4) The Commission shall only exercise the powers provided for in this Article when at least six High Contracting Parties are bound by declarations made in accordance with the preceding paragraphs.

Article 26. The Commission may only deal with the matter after all domestic remedies have been exhausted, according to the generally recognized rules of international law, and within a period of six months from the date on which the final decision was taken.

Article 27. (1) The Commission shall not deal with any petition submitted under Article 25 which

(*a*) is anonymous, or

(*b*) is substantially the same as a matter which has already been examined by the Commission or has already been submitted to another procedure of international investigation or settlement and if it contains no relevant new information.

(2) The Commission shall consider inadmissible any petition submitted under Article 25 which it considers incompatible with the provisions of the present Convention, manifestly ill-founded, or an abuse of the right of petition.

(3) The Commission shall reject any petition referred to it which it considers inadmissible under Article 26.

Article 28. In the event of the Commission accepting a petition referred to it:

(*a*) it shall, with a view to ascertaining the facts, undertake together with the representatives of the parties an examination of the petition and, if need be, an investigation, for the effective conduct of which the States concerned shall furnish all necessary facilities, after an exchange of views with the Commission;

(*b*) it shall place itself at the disposal of the parties concerned with a view to securing a friendly settlement of the matter on the basis of respect for Human Rights as defined in this Convention.

Article 29. (1) The Commission shall perform the functions set out in Article 28 by means of a Sub-Commission consisting of seven members of the Commission.

(2) Each of the parties concerned may appoint as members of this Sub-Commission a person of its choice.

(3) The remaining members shall be chosen by lot in accordance with arrangements prescribed in the Rules of Procedure of the Commission.

Article 30. If the Sub-Commission succeeds in effecting a friendly settlement in accordance with Article 28, it shall draw up a Report which shall be sent to the States concerned, to the Committee of Ministers and to the Secretary-General of the Council of Europe for publication. This Report shall be confined to a brief statement of the facts and of the solution reached.

Article 31. (1) If a solution is not reached, the Commission shall draw up a Report on the facts and state its opinion as to whether the facts found disclose a breach by the State concerned of its obligations under the Convention. The opinions of all the members of the Commission on this point may be stated in the Report.

(2) The Report shall be transmitted to the Committee of Ministers. It shall also be transmitted to the States concerned, who shall not be at liberty to publish it.

(3) In transmitting the Report to the Committee of Ministers the Commission may make such proposals as it thinks fit.

Article 32. (1) If the question is not referred to the Court in accordance with Article 48 of this Convention within a period of three months from the date of the transmission of the Report to the Committee of Ministers, the Committee of Ministers shall decide by a majority of two thirds of the members entitled to sit on the Committee whether there has been a violation of the Convention.

(2) In the affirmative case the Committee of Ministers shall prescribe a period during which the Contracting Party concerned must take the measures required by the decision of the Committee of Ministers.

(3) If the High Contracting Party concerned has not taken satisfactory measures within the prescribed period, the Committee of Ministers shall decide by the majority provided for in paragraph (1) above what effect shall be given to its original decision and shall publish the Report.

(4) The High Contracting Parties undertake to regard as binding on them any decision which the Committee of Ministers may take in application of the preceding paragraphs.

Article 33. The Commission shall meet in camera.

Article 34. The Commission shall take its decisions by a majority of the Members present and voting; the Sub-Commission shall take its decisions by a majority of its Members.

Article 35. The Commission shall meet as the circumstances require. The meetings shall be convened by the Secretary-General of the Council of Europe.

Article 36. The Commission shall draw up its own rules of procedure.

Article 37. The secretariat of the Commission shall be provided by the Secretary-General of the Council of Europe.

SECTION IV

Article 38. The European Court of Human Rights shall consist of a number of judges equal to that of the Members of the Council of Europe. No two judges may be nationals of the same State.

Article 39. (1) The members of the Court shall be elected by the Consultative Assembly by a majority of the votes cast from a list of persons nominated by the Members of the Council of Europe; each Member shall nominate three candidates, of whom two at least shall be its nationals.

(2) As far as applicable, the same procedure shall be followed to complete the Court in the event of the admission of new members of the Council of Europe, and in filling casual vacancies.

(3) The candidates shall be of high moral character and must either possess the qualifications required for appointment to high judicial office or be jurisconsults of recognized competence.

Article 40. (1) The members of the Court shall be elected for a period of nine years. They may be re-elected. However, of the members elected at the first election the terms of four members shall expire at the end of three years, and the terms of four more members shall expire at the end of six years.

(2) The members whose terms are to expire at the end of the initial periods of three and six years shall be chosen by lot by the Secretary-General immediately after the first election has been completed.

(3) A member of the Court elected to replace a member whose term of office has not expired shall hold office for the remainder of his predecessor's term.

(4) The members of the Court shall hold office until replaced. After having been replaced, they shall continue to deal with such cases as they already have under consideration.

Article 41. The Court shall elect its President and Vice-President for a period of three years. They may be re-elected.

Article 42. The members of the Court shall receive for each day of duty a compensation to be determined by the Committee of Ministers.

Article 43. For the consideration of each case brought before it the Court shall consist of a Chamber composed of seven judges. There shall sit as an ex officio member of the Chamber the judge who is a national of any State party concerned, or, if there is none, a person of its choice who shall sit in the capacity of judge; the names of the other judges shall be chosen by lot by the President before the opening of the case.

Article 44. Only the High Contracting Parties and the Commission shall have the right to bring a case before the Court.

Article 45. The jurisdiction of the Court shall extend to all cases concerning the interpretation and application of the present Convention which the High Contracting Parties or the Commission shall refer to it in accordance with Article 48.

Article 46. (1) Any of the High Contracting Parties may at any time declare that it recognizes as compulsory *ipso facto* and without special agreement the jurisdiction of the Court in all matters concerning the interpretation and application of the present Convention.

(2) The declarations referred to above may be made unconditionally or on condition of reciprocity on the part of several or certain other High Contracting Parties or for a specified period.

(3) These declarations shall be deposited with the Secretary-General of the Council of Europe who shall transmit copies thereof to the High Contracting Parties.

Article 47. The Court may only deal with a case after the Commission has acknowledged the failure of efforts for a friendly settlement and within the period of three months provided for in Article 32.

Article 48. The following may bring a case before the Court, provided that the High Contracting Party concerned, if there is only one, or the High Contracting Parties concerned, if there is more than one, are subject to the compulsory jurisdiction of the Court or, failing that, with the consent of the High Contracting Party concerned, if there is only one, or of the High Contracting Parties concerned, if there is more than one:

(*a*) the Commission;

(*b*) a High Contracting Party whose national is alleged to be a victim;

(*c*) a High Contracting Party which referred the case to the Commission;

(*d*) a High Contracting Party against which the complaint has been lodged.

Article 49. In the event of dispute as to whether the Court has jurisdiction, the matter shall be settled by the decision of the Court.

Article 50. If the Court finds that a decision or a measure taken by a legal authority or any other authority of a High Contracting Party, is completely or partially in conflict with the obligations arising from the present Convention, and if the internal law of the said Party allows only partial reparation to be made for the consequences of this decision or measure, the decision of the Court shall, if necessary, afford just satisfaction to the injured party.

Article 51. (1) Reasons shall be given for the judgment of the Court.

(2) If the judgment does not represent in whole or in part the unanimous opinion of the judges, any judge shall be entitled to deliver a separate opinion.

Article 52. The judgment of the Court shall be final.

Article 53. The High Contracting Parties undertake to abide by the decision of the Court in any case to which they are parties.

Article 54. The judgment of the Court shall be transmitted to the Committee of Ministers which shall supervise its execution.

Article 55. The Court shall draw up its own rules and shall determine its own procedure.

Article 56. (1) The first election of the members of the Court shall take place after the declarations by the High Contracting Parties mentioned in Article 46 have reached a total of eight.

(2) No case can be brought before the Court before this election.

SECTION V

Article 57. On receipt of a request from the Secretary-General of the Council of Europe any High Contracting Party shall furnish an explanation of the manner in which its internal law ensures the effective implementation of any of the provisions of this Convention.

Article 58. The expenses of the Commission and the Court shall be borne by the Council of Europe.

Article 59. The members of the Commission and of the Court shall be entitled, during the discharge of their functions, to the privileges and immunities provided for in Article 40 of the Statute of the Council of Europe and in the agreements made thereunder.

Article 60. Nothing in this Convention shall be construed as limiting or derogating from any of the human rights and fundamental freedoms which may be ensured under the laws of any High Contracting Party or under any other agreement to which it is a Party.

Article 61. Nothing in this Convention shall prejudice the powers conferred on the Committee of Ministers by the Statute of the Council of Europe.

Article 62. The High Contracting Parties agree that, except by special agreement, they will not avail themselves of treaties, conventions or declarations in force between them for the purpose of submitting, by way of petition, a dispute arising out of the interpretation or application of this Convention to a means of settlement other than those provided for in this Convention.

Article 63. (1) Any State may at the time of its ratification or at any time thereafter declare by notification addressed to the Secretary-General of the Council of Europe that the present Convention shall extend to all or any of the territories for whose international relations it is responsible.

(2) The Convention shall extend to the territory or territories named in the notification as from the thirtieth day after the receipt of this notification by the Secretary-General of the Council of Europe.

(3) The provisions of this Convention shall be applied in such territories with due regard, however, to local requirements.

(4) Any State which has made a declaration in accordance with Paragraph 1 of this Article may at any time thereafter declare on behalf of one or more of the territories to which the declaration relates that it accepts the competence of the Commission to receive petitions from individuals, non-governmental organizations or groups of individuals in accordance with Article 25 of the present Convention.

Article 64. (1) Any State may, when signing this Convention or when depositing its instrument of ratification, make a reservation in respect of any particular provision of the Convention to the extent that any law then in force in its territory is not in conformity with the provision. Reservations of a general character shall not be permitted under this Article.

(2) Any reservation made under this Article shall contain a brief statement of the law concerned.

Article 65. (1) A High Contracting Party may denounce the present Convention only after the expiry of five years from the date on which it became a Party to it and after six months notice contained in a notification addressed to the Secretary-General of the Council of Europe, who shall inform the other High Contracting Parties.

(2) Such a denunciation shall not have the effect of releasing the High Contracting Party concerned from its obligations under this Convention in respect of any act which, being capable of constituting a violation of such obligations, may have been performed by it before the date at which the denunciation became effective.

(3) Any High Contracting Party which shall cease to be a Member of the Council of Europe shall cease to be a Party to this Convention under the same conditions.

(4) The Convention may be denounced in accordance with the provisions of the preceding paragraphs in respect of any territory to which it has been declared to extend under the terms of Article 63.

Article 66. (1) This Convention shall be open to the signature of the Members of the Council of Europe. It shall be ratified. Ratifications shall be deposited with the Secretary-General of the Council of Europe.

(2) The present Convention shall come into force after the deposit of ten instruments of ratification.

(3) As regards any signatory ratifying subsequently, the Convention shall come into force at the date of the deposit of its instrument of ratification.

(4) The Secretary-General of the Council of Europe shall notify all the Members of the Council of Europe of the entry into force of the Convention, the names of the High Contracting Parties who have ratified it, and the deposit of all instruments of ratification which may be effected subsequently.

DONE at Rome this 4th day of November, 1950, in English and French, both texts being equally authentic, in a single copy which shall remain deposited in the archives of the Council of Europe. The Secretary-General shall transmit certified copies to each of the signatories.

Ratifications

Austria	3 September 1958
Belgium	14 June 1955
Denmark	13 April 1953
Federal Republic of Germany	5 December 1952
Greece	28 March 1953
Iceland	29 June 1953
Ireland	25 February 1953
Italy	26 October 1955
Luxemburg	3 September 1953
Netherlands	31 August 1954*
Norway	15 January 1952
Sweden	4 February 1952
Turkey	18 May 1954
United Kingdom	8 March 1951†

Entry into Force
3 September 1953

PROTOCOL TO THE CONVENTION ON HUMAN RIGHTS

Signed in Paris on 20 March 1952

The Governments signatory hereto, being Members of the Council of Europe,

Being resolved to take steps to ensure the collective enforcement of certain rights and freedoms other than those already included in Section I of the Convention for the Protection of Human Rights and Fundamental Freedoms signed at Rome on 4th November, 1950 (hereinafter referred to as 'the Convention'),

Have agreed as follows:

Article 1. Every natural or legal person is entitled to the peaceful enjoyment of his possessions. No one shall be deprived of his

*The Convention, with the exception of Article 6, paragraph 3 (*c*), and the Protocol were extended on 1 December 1955 to Surinam and the Netherlands Antilles.

† The Convention was extended to 42 territories on 23 October, 1953.

possessions except in the public interest and subject to the conditions provided for by law and by the general principles of international law.

The preceding provisions shall not, however, in any way impair the right of a State to enforce such laws as it deems necessary to control the use of property in accordance with the general interest or to secure the payment of taxes or other contributions or penalties.

Article 2. No person shall be denied the right to education. In the exercise of any functions which it assumes in relation to education and to teaching, the State shall respect the right of parents to ensure such education and teaching in conformity with their own religious and philosophical convictions.

Article 3. The High Contracting Parties undertake to hold free elections at reasonable intervals by secret ballot, under conditions which will ensure the free expression of the opinion of the people in the choice of the legislature.

Article 4. Any High Contracting Party may at the time of signature or ratification or at any time thereafter communicate to the Secretary-General of the Council of Europe a declaration stating the extent to which it undertakes that the provisions of the present Protocol shall apply to such of the territories for the international relations of which it is responsible as are named therein.

Any High Contracting Party which has communicated a declaration in virtue of the preceding paragraph may from time to time communicate a further declaration modifying the terms of any former declaration or terminating the application of the provisions of this Protocol in respect of any territory.

A declaration made in accordance with this Article shall be deemed to have been made in accordance with Paragraph (1) of Article 63 of the Convention.

Article 5. As between the High Contracting Parties the provisions of Articles 1, 2, 3 and 4 of this Protocol shall be regarded as additional Articles to the Convention and all the provisions of the Convention shall apply accordingly.

Article 6. This Protocol shall be open for signature by the Members of the Council of Europe, who are the signatories of the Convention; it shall be ratified at the same time as or after the ratification of the Convention. It shall enter into force after the deposit of ten instruments of ratification. As regards any signatory ratifying subsequently, the Protocol shall enter into force at the date of the deposit of its instrument of ratification.

The instruments of ratification shall be deposited with the Secretary-General of the Council of Europe, who will notify all Members of the names of those who have ratified.

DONE at Paris on the 20th day of March 1952, in English and French, both texts being equally authentic, in a single copy which shall remain deposited in the archives of the Council of Europe. The Secretary-General shall transmit certified copies to each of the signatory Governments.

Ratifications

Austria	3 September 1958
Belgium	14 June 1955
Denmark	13 April 1953
Federal Republic of Germany	13 February 1957
Greece	28 March 1953
Iceland	29 June 1953
Ireland	25 February 1953
Italy	26 October 1955
Luxemburg	3 September 1953
Netherlands	31 August 1954
Norway	18 December 1952
Sweden	22 June 1953
Turkey	18 May 1954
United Kingdom	3 November 1952

Entry into Force
18 May 1954

Constitution of Belgium

7 February 1831
(With Amendments)

TITLE II
BELGIAN CITIZENS AND THEIR RIGHTS

Article 4. Belgian nationality is acquired, retained, and lost according to regulations established by the civil law.

The present Constitution and the other laws relating to political rights determine what other conditions are necessary for the exercise of these rights.

Article 5. Naturalization is granted by the legislative power.

Full naturalization alone admits foreigners to equality with Belgians in the exercise of political rights.

Article 6. There shall be no distinction of classes* in the state.

All Belgians are equal before the law; they alone are admissible to civil and military offices, with such exceptions as may be established by law for particular cases.

Article 7. Individual liberty is guaranteed.

No one may be prosecuted except in cases provided for by law and in the form therein prescribed.

Except when one is taken in the commission of an offence, no one may be arrested without a warrant issued by a magistrate, notice of which must be given at the time of arrest, or at the latest within twenty-four hours thereafter.

Article 8. No person shall be removed against his will from the jurisdiction of the judge to whom the law assigns him.

*The French text is 'Il n'y a dans l'État aucune distinction d'ordres'. This is a reference to the old divisions of the State into three orders: nobility, clergy, and *tiers état*.

Article 9. No penalty shall be established or enforced except by virtue of a law.

Article 10. The private domicile is inviolable; no search of premises shall take place except in the cases provided for by law and according to the form therein prescribed.

Article 11. No one may be deprived of his property except for a public purpose and according to the forms established by law, and in consideration of a just compensation previously determined.

Article 12. Punishment by confiscation of property shall not be established.

Article 13. Total deprivation of civil rights (*mort civile*) is abolished and shall not be re-established.

Article 14. Religious liberty and the freedom of public worship, as well as free expression of opinion in all matters, are guaranteed with the reservation of power to suppress offences committed in the use of these liberties.

Article 15. No one shall be compelled to join in any manner whatever in the forms and ceremonies of any religious worship, nor to observe its days of rest.

Article 16. The State shall not interfere either in the appointment or in the installation of the ministers of any religious denomination whatever, nor shall it forbid them to correspond with their superiors or to publish their proceedings, subject, in the latter case, to the ordinary responsibility of the press and of publication.

Civil marriage shall always precede the religious ceremony, except in cases to be established by law if found necessary.

Article 17. Private instruction shall not be restricted; all measures interfering with it are forbidden; the repression of offences shall be regulated by law.

Public instruction given at the expense of the State shall likewise be regulated by law.

Article 18. The press is free; no censorship shall ever be established; no security shall be exacted of writers, publishers, or printers.*

In case the writer is known and is a resident of Belgium, the publisher, printer, or distributor shall not be prosecuted.

Article 19. Belgians have the right, without previous authorization, to assemble peaceably and without arms, conforming themselves to the laws which regulate the exercise of this right.

This provision does not apply to assemblies in the open air, which remain entirely under the police laws.

Article 20. Belgians have the right of association; this right shall not be restricted by any preventive measure.

Article 21. Anyone has the right to address petitions to the public authorities, signed by one or more persons.

Legally organized bodies alone have the right to petition under a collective name.

Article 22. The privacy of correspondence is inviolable. The law shall determine who are the agents responsible for the violation of the secrecy of letters entrusted to the post.

Article 23. The use of the languages spoken in Belgium is optional. This matter may be regulated only by law and only for acts of public authority and for judicial proceedings.

Article 24. No previous authorization is necessary to bring action against public officials for the acts of their administration, except as provided for Ministers.

*Articles 96 and 98, not reprinted here, relate to trials of offences of the press.

Declaration of the Rights of Man and of the Citizen*

26 August 1789

Article 1. Men are born and remain free and equal in respect of rights. Social distinctions shall be based solely upon public utility.

Article 2. The purpose of all civil associations is the preservation of the natural and imprescriptible rights of man. These rights are liberty, property, security, and resistance to oppression.

Article 3. The nation is essentially the source of all sovereignty; nor shall any body of men or any individual exercise authority which is not expressly derived from it.

Article 4. Liberty consists in the power of doing whatever does not injure another. Accordingly, the exercise of the natural rights of every man has no other limits than those which are necessary to secure to every other man the free exercise of the same rights; and these limits are determinable only by the law.

Article 5. The law ought to prohibit only actions hurtful to society. What is not prohibited by the law should not be hindered; nor should any one be compelled to do that which the law does not require.

Article 6. The law is an expression of the common will. All citizens have a right to concur, either personally or by their representation, in its formation. It should be the same for all, whether it protects or punishes; and all, being equal in its sight, are equally eligible to all honours, places, and employments, according to their different abilities. without any other distinction than that of their virtues and talents.

*English translation in R. Helleu, *France-Amerique 1776–1789–1917*, Paris, 1918.

Article 7. No one shall be accused, arrested, or imprisoned, save in the cases determined by law, and according to the forms which it has prescribed. All who solicit, promote, execute, or cause to be executed, arbitrary orders, ought to be punished, and every citizen summoned or apprehended by virtue of the law, ought immediately to obey, and becomes culpable if he resists.

Article 8. The law should impose only such penalties as are absolutely and evidently necessary; and no one ought to be punished but by virtue of a law promulgated before the offence, and legally applied.

Article 9. Every man being counted innocent until he has been convicted, whenever his arrest becomes indispensable, all rigour more than is necessary to secure his person ought to be provided against by law.

Article 10. No man is to be interfered with because of his opinions, not even because of religious opinions, provided his avowal of them does not disturb public order as established by law.

Article 11. The unrestrained communication of thoughts or opinions being one of the most precious rights of man, every citizen may speak, write and publish freely, provided he be responsible for the abuse of this liberty, in the cases determined by law.

Article 12. A public force being necessary to give security to the rights of men and of citizens, that force is instituted for the benefit of the community, and not for the particular benefit of the person to whom it is entrusted.

Article 13. A common contribution being necessary for the support of the public force, and for defraying the other expenses of government, it should be divided equally among the members of the community, according to their abilities.

Article 14. Every citizen has a right, either of himself or his representative, to a free voice in determining the necessity of public contributions, the appropriation of them, and their amount, mode of assessment, and duration.

Article 15. The community has the right to demand of all its agents an account of their conduct.

Article 16. Every community in which a security of rights and a separation of powers is not provided for needs a constitution.

Article 17. The right to property being inviolable and sacred, no one shall be deprived of it, except in cases of evident public necessity, legally ascertained, and on condition of a previous just indemnity.

Extracts from the French Constitution of 1958

Article 9. The President of the Republic shall preside over the Council of Ministers.

Article 13. The President of the Republic shall sign the ordinances and decrees decided upon in the Council of Ministers.

He shall make appointments to the civil and military posts of the State.

Councillors of State, the Grand Chancellor of the Legion of Honour, Ambassadors and envoys extraordinary, Master Councillors of the Audit Office, Prefects, representatives of the Government in the Overseas Territories, general officers, rectors of academies [regional divisions of the public educational system] and directors of central administrations shall be appointed in meetings of the Council of Ministers.

An organic law shall determine the other posts to be filled in meetings of the Council of Ministers, as well as the conditions under which the power of the President of the Republic to make appointments to office may be delegated by him and exercised in his name.

Article 19. The acts of the President of the Republic, other than those provided for under Articles 8 (first paragraph), 11, 12, 16, 18, 54, 56 and 61, shall be countersigned by the Premier and, should circumstances so require, by the appropriate Ministers.

Article 21. The Premier shall direct the operation of the Government. He shall be responsible for national defence. He shall ensure the execution of the laws. Subject to the provisions of Article 13, he shall have regulatory powers and shall make appointments to civil and military posts.

He may delegate certain of his powers to the Ministers.

He shall replace, should the occasion arise, the President of the

Republic as chairman of the councils and committees provided for under Article 15.

He may, in exceptional instances, replace him as chairman of a meeting of the Council of Ministers by virtue of an explicit delegation and for a specific agenda.

Article 22. The acts of the Premier shall be countersigned, when circumstances so require, by the Ministers responsible for their execution.

Extracts from the Basic Law of the Federal Republic of Germany

Article 1. (1) The dignity of man shall be inviolable. To respect and protect it shall be the duty of all state authority.

(2) The German people therefore acknowledges inviolable and inalienable human rights as the basis of every human community, of peace and of justice in the world.

(3) The following basic rights shall be binding as directly valid law on legislation, administration and judiciary.

Article 2. (1) Everyone shall have the right to the free development of his personality insofar as he does not infringe the rights of others or offend against the constitutional order or the moral code.

(2) Everyone shall have the right to life and physical inviolability. The freedom of the individual shall be inviolable. These rights may be interfered with only on the basis of a law.

Article 3. (1) All men shall be equal before the law.

(2) Men and women shall have equal rights.

(3) No one may be prejudiced or privileged because of his sex, descent, race, language, homeland and origin, faith or his religious and political opinions.

Article 4. (1) Freedom of faith and conscience and freedom of religious and ideological (*weltanschauliche*) profession shall be inviolable.

(2) Undisturbed practice of religion shall be guaranteed.

(3) No one may be compelled against his conscience to perform war service as a combatant. Details shall be regulated by a federal law.

Article 5. (1) Everyone shall have the right freely to express and to disseminate his opinion through speech, writing and illustration and, without hindrance, to instruct himself from generally accessible sources. Freedom of the press and freedom of reporting by radio and motion pictures shall be guaranteed. There shall be no censorship.

(2) These rights shall be limited by the provisions of the general laws, the legal regulations for the protection of juveniles and by the right of personal honour.

(3) Art and science, research and teaching shall be free. Freedom of teaching shall not absolve from loyalty to the constitution.

Article 6. (1) Marriage and family shall be under the special protection of the State.

(2) The care and upbringing of children shall be the natural right of parents and the supreme duty incumbent upon them. The State shall watch over their activity.

(3) Children may be separated from the family against the will of those entitled to bring them up only on a legal basis if those so entitled fail to do their duty or if, on other grounds, a danger of the children being neglected arises.

(4) Every mother shall have a claim to the protection and care of the community.

(5) Illegitimate children shall, through legislation, be given the same conditions for their physical and spiritual development and their position in society as legitimate children.

Article 7. (1) The entire educational system shall be under the supervision of the State.

(2) Those entitled to bring up the child shall have the right to decide whether it shall receive religious instruction.

(3) Religious instruction shall form part of the curriculum in the state schools with the exception of non-confessional schools. Religious instruction shall, without prejudice to the State's right of supervision, be given according to the principles of the religious societies. No teacher may be obliged against his will to give religious instruction.

(4) The right to establish private schools shall be guaranteed. Private schools as substitute for state schools shall require the sanction of the State and shall be subject to Land legislation.

The sanction must be given if the private schools, in their educational aims and facilities, as well as in the scholarly training of their teaching personnel, are not inferior to the state schools and if a separation of the pupils according to the means of the parents is not encouraged. The sanction must be withheld if the economic and legal status of the teaching personnel is not sufficiently assured.

(5) A private elementary school shall be permitted only if the educational administration recognizes a specific pedagogic interest or, at the request of those entitled to bring up children, if it is to be established as a general community school (*Gemeinschaftsschule*), as a confessional or ideological school or if a state elementary school of this type does not exist in the Gemeinde.

(6) Preparatory schools shall remain abolished.

Article 8. (1) All Germans shall have the right, without prior notification or permission, to assemble peacefully and unarmed.

(2) For open air meetings this right may be restricted by legislation or on the basis of a law.

Article 9. (1) All Germans shall have the right to form associations and societies.

(2) Associations, the objects or activities of which conflict with the criminal laws or which are directed against the constitutional order or the concept of international understanding, shall be prohibited.

(3) The right to form associations to safeguard and improve working and economic conditions shall be guaranteed to everyone and to all professions. Agreements which seek to restrict or hinder this right shall be null and void; measures directed to this end shall be illegal.

Article 10. Secrecy of the mail as well as secrecy of the post and tele-communications shall be inviolable. Restrictions may be ordered only on the basis of a law.

Article 11. (1) All Germans shall enjoy freedom of movement throughout the federal territory.

(2) This right may be restricted only by legislation and only for the cases in which an adequate basis of existence is absent and, as a result, particular burdens would arise for the general public or in which it is necessary for the protection of juveniles from neglect, for combating the danger of epidemics or in order to prevent criminal acts.

Article 12. (1) All Germans shall have the right to freely choose their occupation, place of work and place of training. The practice of an occupation may be regulated by legislation.

(2) No one may be compelled to perform a particular kind of work except within the framework of an established general compulsory public service equally applicable to everybody.

(3) Forced labour shall be admissible only in the event of imprisonment ordered by a court.

Article 13. (1) The dwelling shall be inviolable.

(2) Searches may be ordered only by a judge or in the event of imminent danger by other authorities provided by law and may be carried out only in the form prescribed therein.

(3) Interventions and restrictions may otherwise be undertaken only to avert a common danger or mortal danger to individuals and, on the basis of a law, also to prevent imminent danger to public safety and order, especially for the relief of the housing shortage, combating the danger of epidemics or protecting juveniles exposed to dangers.

Article 14. (1) Property and the right of inheritance shall be guaranteed. The contents and limitations shall be determined by legislation.

(2) Property shall involve obligations. Its use shall simultaneously serve the general welfare.

(3) Expropriation shall be admissible only for the well-being of the general public. It may be effected only by legislation or on the basis of a law which shall regulate the nature and extent of compensation. The compensation shall be determined after just consideration of the interests of the general public and the

participants. Regarding the extent of compensation, appeal may be made to the ordinary courts in case of dispute.

Article 15. Land and landed property, natural resources and means of production may, for the purpose of socialization, be transferred to public ownership or other forms of publicly controlled economy by way of a law which shall regulate the nature and extent of compensation. For the compensation, Article 14, paragraph (3), sentences 3 and 4, shall apply appropriately.

Article 16. (1) No one may be deprived of his German citizenship. The loss of citizenship may occur only on the basis of a law and, against the will of the person concerned, only if the person concerned is not rendered stateless thereby.

(2) No German may be extradited to a foreign country. The politically persecuted shall enjoy the right of asylum.

Article 17. Everyone shall have the right, individually or jointly with others, to address written requests or complaints to the competent authorities and to the popular representative bodies.

Article 18. Whoever abuses the freedom of expression of opinion, in particular the freedom of the press (Article 5, paragraph (1)), the freedom of teaching (Article 5, paragraph (3)), the freedom of assembly (Article 8), the freedom of association (Article 9), the secrecy of mail, post and tele-communications (Article 10), property (Article 14), or the right of asylum (Article 16, paragraph (2)), in order to attack the free, democratic basic order, shall forfeit these basic rights. The forfeiture and its extent shall be pronounced by the Federal Constitutional Court.

Article 19. (1) Insofar as according to this Basic Law a basic right may be restricted by legislation or on the basis of a law, the law must apply in general and not solely to the individual case. Furthermore, the law must name the basic right, indicating the Article.

(2) In no case may a basic right be affected in its basic content.

(3) The basic rights shall also apply to juridical persons within

the country insofar as, according to their nature, they may be applied to such persons.

(4) Should any person's rights be infringed by public authority, he may appeal to the courts. Insofar as another authority is not competent, the appeal shall go to the ordinary courts.

Article 4. Liberty consists in the power of doing whatever does not injure another. Accordingly, the exercise of the natural rights of every man has no other limits than those which are necessary to secure to every other man the free exercise of the same rights; and these limits are determinable only by the law.

Article 20. The Federal Republic of Germany is a democratic and social federal State.

All state authority emanates from the people. It shall be exercised by the people by means of elections and voting and by separate legislative, executive and judicial organs. Legislation shall be subject to the constitutional order; the Executive and the Judiciary shall be bound by the law.

Article 80. (1) The Federal Government, a Federal Minister or the Land Government may be authorized by a law to issue ordinances having the force of law (*Rechtsverordnungen*). The content, purpose and scope of the powers conferred must be set forth in the law. The legal basis must be stated in the ordinance. If a law provides that a power may be further delegated, an ordinance having the force of law shall be necessary in order to delegate the powers.

Article 105. (1) and (2) The Federation shall have the exclusive power to legislate on customs matters and fiscal monopolies.

The Federation shall have concurrent power to legislate on:

(1) excise taxes and taxes on transport, motor-vehicles, and transactions (*Verkehrsteuern*), with the exception of taxes with localized application, in particular of real estate acquisition tax, increment value tax, and fire protection tax;

(2) taxes on income, on property, on inheritances, and on donations;

(3) taxes on real estate and business (*Realsteuern*) with the exception of the fixing of tax rates, if it claims the taxes in whole or in part to cover federal expenditure or if the conditions laid down in Article 72, paragraph 2 exist.

Article 106. (1) The yield of fiscal monopolies and receipts from the following taxes shall accrue to the Federation:

(1) customs duties,

(2) such excise taxes as do not accrue to the Länder in accordance with paragraph 2,

(3) turnover tax,

(4) transportation tax,

(5) non-recurrent levies on property, and equalization taxes imposed for the purpose of implementing the Equalization of Burdens legislation,

(6) Berlin emergency aid tax,

(7) income and incorporations surtaxes.

Article 108. (1) Customs duties, fiscal monopolies, excise taxes, subject to concurrent legislative powers, transportation tax, turnover tax, and non-recurrent levies on property shall be administered by federal revenue authorities. The organization of the authorities and the procedure to be applied by them shall be regulated by federal law. The heads of the authorities at intermediate level shall be appointed after consultation of the Land Governments. The Federation may transfer the administration of non-recurrent levies on property to the Land revenue authorities as its agents.

Article 129. (1) and (3) In so far as legal provisions which continue in force as federal law contain an authorization to issue ordinances having the force of law (*Rechtsverordnungen*) or general administrative rules or to perform administrative acts, the authorization shall pass to the agencies henceforth competent in the matter. In cases of doubt, the Federal Government shall decide in agreement with the Bundesrat; the decision must be published.

In so far as legal provisions within the meaning of paragraphs

1 and 2 authorize their amendment or supplementation or the issue of legal provisions instead of laws, these authorizations have expired.

Index

MORE ABOUT PENGUINS
AND PELICANS

Penguinews, which appears every month, contains details of all the new books issued by Penguins as they are published. From time to time it is supplemented by *Penguins in Print* – a complete list of all our available titles. (There are well over three thousand of these.)

A specimen copy of *Penguinews* will be sent to you free on request, and you can become a subscriber for the price of the postage – 4s. for a year's issues (including the complete lists). Just write to Dept EP, Penguin Books Ltd, Harmondsworth, Middlesex, enclosing a cheque or postal order, and your name will be added to the mailing list.

Note: *Penguinews* and *Penguins in Print* are not available in the U.S.A. or Canada

SCIENCE AND TECHNOLOGY
IN EUROPE

Edited by Eric Moonman

In an expanding industrial world where size often means success, Europe is still straddled by two technological super-powers, the United States and Russia. Only by pooling national resources and by large-scale collaboration can we compete on equal terms. In this Penguin Special a group of experts shows how international cooperation can work in several key European industries such as computers, steel, aircraft, space research, chemicals, automation and atomic energy. Their essays are an anatomy of the growing-pains of a new Europe: for in its thorough going re-organization of industry the new technology without frontiers will re-write international and company law, break down unproductive barriers between technology and science in the universities, radically affect the European interests of America and Russia, and even change the structure of European politics. This book confidently predicts the future of science and technology in Europe; but in its implications it goes much farther.